全国职业技能英语系列教材

邮 政 英 语

主　编：王小平　葛蕴鲜
副主编：吴　芳　闫桂娥　张丽辉　彭朝霞　杜昱伟
编　者：马　莉　王小平　王雨莲　刘云霞　朱立刚
　　　　许艳敏　吴　芳　张　红　张丽辉　张京涛
　　　　张　震　杜昱伟　闫桂娥　武　峰　赵荣改
　　　　赵素娟　崔新娟　彭朝霞　智文静　葛兆爽
　　　　葛蕴鲜　董国栋

图书在版编目(CIP)数据

邮政英语/王小平,葛蕴鲜主编.—北京:北京大学出版社,2010.8
(全国职业技能英语系列教材)
ISBN 978-7-301-17698-6

Ⅰ.①邮… Ⅱ.①王…②葛… Ⅲ.①邮政－英语－高等学校:技术学校－教材 Ⅳ.①H31

中国版本图书馆 CIP 数据核字(2010)第 167309 号

书　　　名：邮政英语
著作责任者：王小平　葛蕴鲜　主编
责任编辑：李　颖
标准书号：ISBN 978-7-301-17698-6/H・2625
出版发行：北京大学出版社
地　　　址：北京市海淀区成府路 205 号　100871
网　　　址：http://www.pup.cn　电子信箱:zpup@pup.pku.edu.cn
电　　　话：邮购部 62752015　发行部 62750672　编辑部 62754382　出版部 62754962
印　刷　者：北京大学印刷厂
经　销　者：新华书店
　　　　　　787 毫米×1092 毫米　16 开本　8.5 印张　180 千字
　　　　　　2010 年 8 月第 1 版　2019 年 5 月第 7 次印刷
定　　　价：36.00 元

未经许可,不得以任何方式复制或抄袭本书之部分或全部内容。
版权所有,侵权必究
举报电话:(010)62752024　电子信箱:fd@pup.pku.edu.cn

全国职业技能英语系列教材

编委会

顾问

胡壮麟（北京大学）　　　刘黛琳（中央广播电视大学）

总主编

丁国声（河北外国语职业学院）

编委会名单（以姓氏笔画为序）

丁小莉（山东商业职业学院）
王乃彦（天津对外经济贸易职业学院）
牛　健（中央广播电视大学）
伍忠杰（电子科技大学）
李相敏（河北外国语职业学院）
李恩亮（江苏海事职业技术学院）
张　冰（北京大学出版社）
张九明（开封大学）
张春生（衡水职业技术学院）
陆松岩（江苏城市职业学院）
陈玉华（成都航空职业学院）
林晓琴（重庆电力高等专科学校）
赵　倩（重庆机电职业技术学院）
赵　鹏（北京联合大学）
赵爱萍（浙江水利水电专科学校）
赵翠华（承德民族师范高等专科学校）
胡海青（南京交通职业技术学院）
贾　方（辽宁装备制造职业技术学院）
黄宗英（北京联合大学）
崔秀敏（承德石油高等专科学校）
蒋　磊（河南商业高等专科学校）
程　亚（江西景德镇陶瓷学院）
黎富玉（成都航空职业学院）
潘月洲（南京工业职业技术学院）
Martin Fielko（Cornelsen Press GmbH & Co. KG）

总 序

我国高职高专教育的春天来到了。随着国家对高职高专教育重视程度的加深,职业技能教材体系的建设成为了当务之急。高职高专过去沿用和压缩大学本科教材的时代一去不复返了。

语言学家 Harmer 指出:"如果我们希望学生学到的语言是在真实生活中能够使用的语言,那么在教材编写中接受技能和产出技能的培养也应该像在生活中那样有机地结合在一起。"

教改的关键在教师,教师的关键在教材,教材的关键在理念。我们依据《高职高专教育英语课程教学基本要求》的精神和编者做了大量调查,秉承"实用为主,够用为度,学以致用,触类旁通"的原则,历经两年艰辛,为高职高专学生编写了这套专业技能课和实训课的英语教材。

本套教材的内容贴近工作岗位,突出岗位情景英语,是一套职场英语教材,具有很强的实用性、仿真性、职业性,其特色体现在以下几个方面:

1. 开放性

   本套教材在坚持编写理念、原则及体例的前提下,不断增加新的行业或岗位技能英语分册作为教材的延续。

2. 国际性

   本套教材以国内自编为主,以国外引进为辅,取长补短,浑然一体。目前已从德国引进了某些行业的技能英语教材,还将从德国或他国引进优秀教材经过本土化后奉献给广大师生。

3. 职业性

   本套教材是由高职院校教师与行业专家针对具体工作岗位、情景过程共同设计编写。同时注重与行业资格证书相结合。

4. 任务性

   基于完成某岗位工作任务而需要的英语知识和技能是本套教材的由来与初衷。因此,各分册均以任务型练习为主。

5. 实用性

本教材注重基础词汇的复习和专业词汇的补充。适合于在校最后一学期的英语教学，着重培养和训练学生初步具有与其日后职业生涯所必需的英语交际能力。

本教材在编写过程中，参考和引用了国内外作者的相关资料，得到了北京大学外语编辑部的倾力奉献，在此，一并向他们表示敬意和感谢。由于本套教材是一种创新和尝试，书中瑕疵必定不少，敬请指正。

丁国声

教育部高职高专英语类专业教学指导委员会委员

河北省高校外语教学研究会副会长

河北外国语职业学院院长

2008年6月

编 写 说 明

《邮政英语》教材为高职高专行业英语教学阶段所使用的行业英语教材，它既是基础英语学习阶段的延伸和补充，同时也为专业英语阶段的学习打下基础。本教材主要适用于邮政各专业学生行业英语学习、邮政企业员工行业英语培训和自主学习的使用。

本教材内容涉及邮政行业各业务板块，如：邮务类业务、速递物流业务、金融保险业务、集邮业务等。具体内容包括邮政历史、万国邮联、普遍服务、邮局、投递员、客户服务、集邮、直复营销、速递、物流、邮政技术与设备、邮政金融保险、社会责任和邮政可持续发展等方面的相关知识。

本教材特点：1. 实现基础阶段与行业阶段的有机衔接；2. 将语言学习与职业技能培养有机结合；3. 注重学生职业能力、素质及企业文化内涵的培养；4. 注重选材的针对性、时代性和趣味性。5. 既遵循英语语言教学的客观规律，循序渐进，又按照专业内容的系统性，由浅入深。二者既保持独立性，又能相互兼容，彼此协调。

本教材共分10个单元，每个单元都包括导入、视听、阅读、拓展练习、职业技能、了解邮政、邮政术语等七个板块。

（1）导入（Lead in）

导入板块主要是通过图片或视频引出讨论话题，再以小组讨论的形式引导学习者对单元主题进行初步了解。因此，该板块既是整个单元内容的导入，又可以作为听说训练的热身。

（2）视听（Audio-Visual）

视听板块主要通过视听材料训练学生的听力理解能力。练习内容包括泛听和精听。顺序上泛听在先，精听在后，目的是训练学生正确的听力理解策略，即在听力理解的过程中先理解材料大意，再精听每一个单词。

（3）阅读（Reading）

阅读板块包括两篇阅读材料及相关练习题。围绕每篇阅读材料既设计了课前阅读题，同时还设计了课后练习题。课前阅读题主要从语篇角度进行了设计，内容包括篇章填空、段落大意等题型，由学生在课前预习时完成，目的是训练学生对语篇的把握。课后练习主要训练学生对重点词汇和结构的掌握，包括填空和翻译练习，练习中的句子绝大部分围绕邮政行业英语进行编写。

（4）拓展练习（Extended Practice）

拓展练习板块通过图文并茂的形式和生动有趣的练习，进一步拓展了学生对相关单元邮政词汇、术语的学习，同时开阔了学生的眼界，拓宽了学生对单元主题的了解。

（5）职业技能（Professional Skills）

职业技能板块包括邮政行业从业人员办理国际业务，处理国际邮件所必备的基本技能训练，其中"窗口英语会话"、"英文地址书写""英文地址批译"、"英文国名识读"等训练贯穿教材始终。通过将学生置于真实行业环境下，进行有针对性的行业英语技能训练，培养他们处理真实任务、解决真正问题的能力，使学生达到邮政行业相关业务能力要求，毕业后能够很快胜任相关工作。

（6）了解邮政（Get to Know the Post）

了解邮政板块介绍了邮政行业相关文化常识，包括世界邮政日、邮政标示、普遍服务、黑便士邮票、直邮历史、速递历史、圣诞老人邮政编码、古代驿使图以及绿色邮政等内容。在提高学生英语语言水平、邮政英语水平的同时，使学生更加了解邮政、热爱邮政，同时提升和加强学生的综合素质和企业文化内涵，为学生今后的可持续发展奠定基础。

（7）邮政术语（Do it Yourself）

邮政术语以学生动手自己制作邮政英语专业术语卡片的形式，充分发挥学生主观能动性。通过学生自己对所学单元邮政术语的回顾和总结，既掌握了邮政术语中英文表达形式，同时还锻炼了总结和归纳能力。

以上各板块内容在设计上力求达到知识性和趣味性相结合，体现以学生为中心，突出任务教学和自主学习的外语教学理念；既强调英语语言知识的系统学习和训练，同时也注重邮政行业英语相关知识的学习和技能训练。

本教材通过把语言材料进行大量处理，将英语语言知识与行业知识合二为一，将对语言规律的学习融于专业外语的内容之中，实现英语应用能力的培养与职业的密切关联，使学生在掌握英语基础语言知识的同时，熟悉国外邮政在业务、技术、管理、服务等领域的最新发展，了解行业文化，拓展国际视野，掌握更多的职业技能，为学生今后的工作和学习打下良好基础。

本教材编写队伍长期从事基础英语教学和邮政专业英语教学的研究与实践。他们深入企业一线学习、调研、编写、出版了大量邮政英语相关教材，参与编写了邮政职业技能鉴定培训教材，为邮政企业进行了各类邮政英语培训，参与多项教育及邮政课题研究、参与了中国邮政网络培训学院的建设。1997年，所主持的"邮政专业英语教学改革的研究与实践"荣获河北省普通高校教学成果一等奖。可以说本教材是编写组各位成员多年教学和企业实践经验的结晶。

在本教材编写过程中，我们得到了中国邮政相关企业和部门、教育部高等学校高职高专英语类专业教学指导委员会、石家庄邮电职业技术学院有关领导以及北京大学出版社的大力支持；中国邮政集团公司国际合作部、中国邮政速递物流公司、北京市邮政公司、上海市邮政公司、广东省邮政公司、河北省邮政公司、山东省邮政公司、辽宁省邮政公司等在资料搜集和企业调研方面给予了积极帮助；教育部高等学校高职高专英语类专业教学指导委员会委员丁国声院长对本教材给予了积极指导；北京大学出版社李颖编辑为此书出版付出了大量的心血，在此一并表示感谢。

编者
2010年8月

CONTENTS

Unit 1 **The Post** 1

    Reading 1   History of the Post 2
    Reading 2   Universal Postal Union 5

Unit 2 **Post Office** 13

    Reading 1   Post Office of the Royal Mail 14
    Reading 2   Being Your Own Postman 17

Unit 3 **Mail Carrier** 25

    Reading 1   Delivering the Mail 26
    Reading 2   Proud to Serve 29

Unit 4 **Customer Service** 37

    Reading 1   How to Treat Your Customers? 38
    Reading 2   Dealing with Difficult Customers 41

Unit 5 **Philately** 49

    Reading 1   Such a Simple Idea—The Story of the Postage Stamp 50
    Reading 2   The Philatelist's Passion 53

Unit 6 **Direct Marketing** 61

    Reading 1   Mailshots 62
    Reading 2   A Piece that Pops 66

Unit 7 **EMS and Logistics** 71

    Reading 1   TNT Express 72
    Reading 2   UPS Supply Chain Solutions 75

Unit 8	**Postal Technology and Equipment**	85
	Reading 1 Sorting the Mail	86
	Reading 2 The Challenge of Emerging Technologies	88
Unit 9	**Postal Finance and Insurance**	95
	Reading 1 Japan Post Bank	96
	Reading 2 How Does Insurance Work?	99
Unit 10	**Social Responsibility**	107
	Reading 1 Leaving a Green Footprint	109
	Reading 2 Taking Responsibility	112

Unit 1 The Post

 Lead in

1 **The following chart is the journey of domestic mail in Sweden. Please describe it in your own words.**

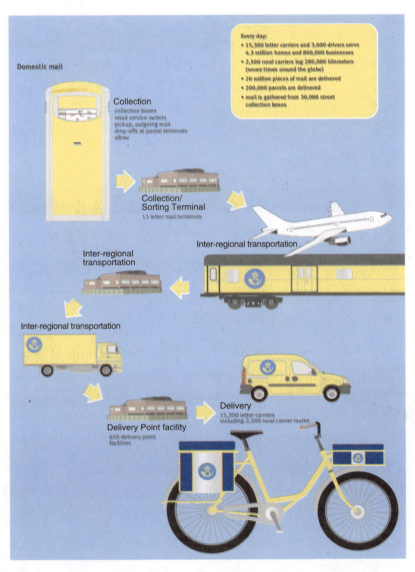

UNIT 1 THE POST

Audio-Visual

2 **Watch the video and answer the following questions.**

1. When and where was the Universal Postal Union established?
2. When is the World Post Day and what does it focus on?
3. What kind of organization is the Universal Postal Union?

3 **Watch the video again and fill out the blanks with what you hear.**

Even in today's (1) _____ age of the Internet and mobile communication, millions of letters and parcels (2) _____ to crisscross the globe everyday of every year. For millions of people, the post remains the most (3) _____ means of communication. Today's global postal network interconnects a vast range of new communication methods, from the (4) _____ of information and goods to the (5) _____ transmission of messages and money. Ensuring the interconnectivity between the world postal services is one (6) _____ — the Universal Postal Union. The UPU serves as (7) _____ global stage for all the players on the postal scene. It facilitates (8) _____ among them and promotes the development of an all-inclusive and genuine universal postal service.

Reading 1

4 **Read the passage below. Fill out the blanks with the following words.**

| brought about | needs | keep pace with | hampered | proposal | bilateral |

History of the Post

The origin of the post is lost in the mists of time. In ancient lands such as China, Persia, Egypt, Greece and the provinces of the Roman Empire, we find traces of a communication system operated by word of mouth or writing and based on relays of men and horses stationed at different points along the highways. The

Vocabulary Assistant

mist n. 薄雾
Greece n. 希腊
trace n. 踪迹，痕迹
station v. 安置，驻扎

Persia n. 波斯（西南亚国家，现在的伊朗）
Roman adj. 罗马的，罗马人的
relay n. 接力，传递

Post as such was the monopoly of monarchs and princes, whose main concern was that their orders should reach the farthest corners of their vast domains. As social life developed, private individuals were allowed to communicate with one another by means of the couriers of princes and monasteries.

This rudimentary organization, half official and half private, lasted until the end of the Middle Ages, but before long it was found to be inadequate to meet the needs of a continually changing society. With the advent of printing, education penetrated into all social strata, while the discovery of new worlds and the consequences of that event extended relations between nations. Thus communications steadily increased. Under the pressure of these needs, the Post inevitably developed. During the sixteenth century, thanks to the impetus given to it by Franz von Taxis, who for the first time created a postal service operating in several European States, it began to extend beyond national frontiers. Later, in the eighteenth century, it definitively became a public service and gradually assumed its present form.

International postal communications were originally governed by _____ agreements which answered the particular _____ of each country. This system, involving a great variety of rates calculated in different currencies and according to different units of weight, made it complicated to operate the service and _____ its development. The invention of steam navigation and the railway _____ a change in the postal system.  The administrations began to realize that, if international communications were to _____ the means of transport, formalities would have to be standardized and reduced. The first step in that direction was taken in Great Britain in 1840. On the _____ of Rowland Hill, the rate for letters in the internal service was reduced to a penny; that reform was accompanied by the creation of the postage stamp.

In 1868, Heinrich von Stephan, a German, drew up the outline of a plan for a postal union of the world. He proposed to his Government that the plan be submitted to a Conference, which, at the invitation of the Swiss Government, met at Berne on 15 September 1874.

Vocabulary Assistant

monopoly n. 垄断,专营服务
prince n. 王子
courier n. 信使，送快信的人
rudimentary adj. 初步的，未发展的
strata n.（pl.）阶层
inevitably adv. 不可避免地，必然地
definitively adv. 确定地，最后地
currency n. 流通，货币
formality n. 正式手续
propose v. 提议，建议

monarch n. 君主，帝王
domain n. 领土，领地
monastery n. 修道院，寺院
penetrate v. 渗透，穿透
steadily adv. 稳定地
impetus n. 推动力，促进
assume v. 呈现（某种形式）
navigation n. 航海，航空
creation n. 创造，产生
submit v. 呈送，提交

5 Pay attention to the italicized parts in the English sentences and translate the Chinese sentences by simulating the structure of the English sentences.

1. *As social life developed*, private individuals *were allowed* to communicate with one another by means of the couriers of princes and monasteries.
   随着社会的发展，私人企业也被允许经营邮电业务。
   _____

2. The administrations *began to realize* that, *if* international communications *were to keep pace with* the means of transport, formalities would have to be standardized and reduced.
   各国邮政开始认识到，如果一个公司要想跟上时代的变化，必须进行一些改革。
   _____

3. *Thanks to* the impetus given to it by Franz von Taxis, who for the first time created a postal service operating in several European States, it *began to extend* beyond national frontiers.
   由于员工的共同努力，这项邮政新业务开办到了偏远地区。
   _____

4. *With the advent of printing*, education penetrated into all social strata, while the discovery of new worlds and the consequences of that event extended relations between nations.
   随着新处理系统的上线，邮件中心的日处理邮件量从以往的1.8万件增至4万件，处理能力大幅提高。
   _____

6 Complete the sentences with the following words, changing the form if necessary.

> consequence   inadequate   submit   concern   penetrate

1. In an era of growing _____ about identity theft, we are doing everything in our power to keep the mail safe and secure.
2. _____ investment in our core infrastructure has left our network in great need of renewal.
3. The Internet, email and other technological advances in communications have reduced lettermail volumes, and as a _____ reduced the economic value of the exclusive privilege.
4. Please _____ your application form to the post office in duplicate.
5. If pests _____ the warehouse, steps must be taken immediately to eliminate them.

Reading 2

7 **Read the passage below. Choose the best title for each numbered paragraph.**

A   The Establishment of UPU
B   The Working Languages of UPU
C   The Organizations of UPU
D   The Functions of UPU
E   The Postal Strategy of UPU
F   The Commemorative Monument of UPU

Universal Postal Union

1   The UPU was established on 9 October 1874 and its headquarters is in Berne, Switzerland. (1) The first Congress which is called Berne Congress resulted in the signing of the 1874 Treaty of Berne, which established the first collective Convention and founded the "General Postal Union". The Convention entered into force on 1 July 1875. Three years later, the title "General Postal Union", was changed to "Universal Postal Union".

2   To celebrate its 25th anniversary, an Extraordinary Congress was held in Berne in July 1900. On the proposal of Germany, that Congress decided to erect a commemorative monument in Berne. Inaugurated on 4 October 1909; the monument was the work of the French sculptor Charles Rene de Saint-Marceaux. The motto of his project was "Around the World". The granite and bronze monument is located in a Berne park to the west of the Federal Palace. It shows five messengers, passing letters round the globe. At the ceremony marking the 75th anniversary of the erection of the monument, Mr. Sobhi, Director-General of the International Bureau, gave an address. As he stated "(2) The five figures representing the five continents are the most sublime expression of the harmony of the peoples in the postal field; they remind us of the reason for the existence of the UPU; the world, a single postal territory".

Vocabulary Assistant

congress *n.* 代表大会
collective *adj.* 集体的
extraordinary *adj.* 非常的，特别的
commemorative *adj.* 纪念的
sculptor *n.* 雕刻家
granite *n.* 花岗岩
bureau *n.* 局
harmony *n.* 和谐

treaty *n.* 条约
convention *n.* 公约
erect *v.* 树立，直立
inaugurate *v.* 举行（落成）典礼
motto *n.* 题词，座右铭
federal *adj.* 联邦的
sublime *adj.* 崇高的，卓越的
territory *n.* 领土，领域

Congress is the supreme body of the Union and consists of the representatives of member countries. (3) Every four years the members of the large postal family meet to revise international postal regulations and to draw up programs of action to deal with the concerns of the moment. Congress has therefore essentially legislative duties. This rule has been broken only because of two world wars: the 1906 Rome Congress and the 1920 Madrid Congress being 14 years apart and the 1939 Buenos Aires Congress and the 1947 Paris Congress being 8 years.

3   The four bodies of the Union are the International Bureau (IB), the Council of Administration (CA), the Postal Operations Council (POC) and the Consultative Committee (CC). IB, the UPU's headquarters, is located in Berne, Switzerland. It serves as an office of liaison, information and consultation, and promotes technical cooperation among Union members. CA ensures the continuity of the UPU's work between Congresses, supervises its activities and studies regulatory, administrative, legislative and legal issues. POC deals with the operational, economic and commercial aspects of international postal services. CC represents the interests of the wider international postal sector, and provides a framework for effective dialogue between postal industry stakeholders. (4) It consists of non-governmental organizations representing customers, delivery service providers, workers' organizations, suppliers of goods and services to the postal sector and other organizations that have an interest in international postal services, including direct marketers, private operators, international mailers and printers.

In 1948 the UPU became a United Nations specialized agency.

Vocabulary Assistant

supreme *adj.* 最高的
legislative *adj.* 立法的
consultative *adj.* 咨询的
continuity *n.* 连续性，连贯性
stakeholder *n.* 利益相关者，股东

revise *v.* 修订，修正
council *n.* 理事会，委员会
liaison *n.* 联络
supervise *v.* 监督

8 Read the above passage again, and translate the underlined sentences into Chinese.

1. _____

2. _____

3. _____

4. _____

9 **Complete the sentences with the following words, changing the form if necessary.**

> revise   commemorative   represent   erect   stakeholder   supervise

1. Japan Post Network properly _____ employees and companies that handle personal data on an outsourcing basis.
2. The survey indicates that there is overwhelming support for the _____ of the Postal Law.
3. Australia Post publishes a quarterly Corporate Responsibility Update newsletter for key _____.
4. As the only official issuer of New Zealand _____ coins, New Zealand Post released five new coin series.
5. On the whole, Itella's logistics volumes _____ the industry's general economic trend.
6. They insisted that Canada Post _____ the new Community Mailboxes on the original site.

Extended Practice

10 **Please put the following names of country in the proper position below its postal logo.**

> Austria   Denmark   Spain   Australia   Britain   Belgium
> Canada   Sweden   Brazil   Korea   Estonia   Egypt
> New Zealand   France   Czech   the Netherlands   the US

Japan

 Professional Skills

11 **The following are expressions used by postal clerks when providing services in the post office. Work in pairs and use these expressions to make conversations.**

邮政服务日常用语 (Postal Service Daily English)

1. 主动提供服务 (Offering Services)
   Hello, can I help you? 您好，您想办理什么业务？
   May I help you, sir? 先生，您想办理什么业务？
   What can I do for you? 我能为您做些什么？
   Anything I can do for you? 我能为您做些什么？
2. 询问是否办理其他业务 (Anything Else?)
   Is that all? 就这些吗？

That's it? 就这些吗?

Anything else? 您还办理其他业务吗?

3. 请对方稍候 (Excusing for a Moment)

One moment, please. 请等一会儿。

Sorry to have kept you waiting. 对不起，让您久等了。

4. 询问邮寄方式 (Ways of Mailing)

How would you like to mail them? 您打算怎么寄?

By airmail? 是寄航空吗?

By surface mail or by airmail? 走水陆路还是走航空?

By ordinary or by registered? 走平信还是走挂号信?

Do you want to insure it? 您要保价/保险吗?

5. 请填单 (Filling in Forms)

Please complete the forms. 请填单。

Please fill in /out the forms. 请填单。

6. 查验内装物品 (Checking Contents)

Would you please show me the contents? 请您把内装物品拿给我看一下好吗?

12 Address the envelope properly with the two addresses below.

Sender: Foreign Language Department
Shijiazhuang Posts and Telecommunications Technical College
318 Tiyu Street
Shijiazhuang, Hebei 050021
P. R. China

Receiver: International Development Unit
Faculty of Education
The University of Melbourne
Victoria 3010
Australia

13 Number the names of the countries or regions according to the map, and translate them into Chinese.

Asia

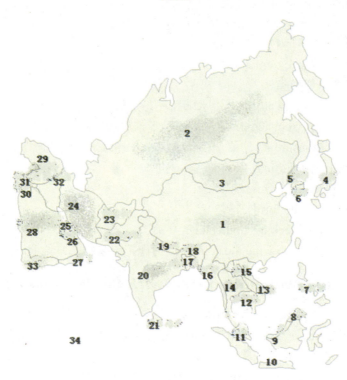

Example:
(1) China _____中国_____   (5) Korea (DPRK) _____朝鲜_____

( ) Brunei _____   ( ) Oman _____
( ) United Arab Emirates _____   ( ) R. O. Korea _____
( ) Sri Lanka _____   ( ) India _____
( ) Afghanistan _____   ( ) Iran _____
( ) Jordan _____   ( ) Pakistan _____
( ) Indonesia _____   ( ) Japan _____
( ) Russia _____   ( ) Qatar _____
( ) the Philippines _____   ( ) Mongolia _____
( ) Malaysia _____   ( ) Singapore _____
( ) Yemen _____   ( ) Saudi Arabia _____
( ) Cambodia _____   ( ) Vietnam _____
( ) Maldives _____   ( ) Lebanon _____
( ) Laos _____   ( ) Syria _____
( ) Myanmar (Burma) _____   ( ) Nepal _____
( ) Thailand _____   ( ) Turkey _____
( ) Bangladesh _____   ( ) Bhutan _____

Get to Know the Post

World Post Day is celebrated each year on 9 October, the anniversary of the establishment of the Universal Postal Union in 1874 in the Swiss Capital, Bern. It was declared World Post Day by the UPU Congress held in Tokyo, Japan in 1969. Since then, countries across the world participate annually in the celebrations. The Posts in many countries use the event to introduce or promote new postal products and services.

In most countries philatelic exhibitions are organized during this period and special stamps and date cancellation marks are issued on 9 October. Other activities include the display of World Post Day posters in post offices and other public places; open days at post offices, mail centres and postal museums; the holding of conferences, seminars and workshops; as well as cultural, sport and other recreation activities.

World Post Day

A World Post Day message from the Director General of the Universal Postal Union is sent each year to all Posts, read during celebrations and published in the media. The UPU in cooperation with UNESCO has, for the past 35 years, organized an International Letter-writing Competition for young people. Most participating Posts use World Post Day to award prizes to the winners of the competition.

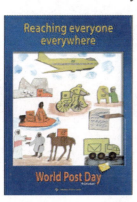

Do It Yourself

Find the English equivalents of the following Chinese from this unit.

Notebook

邮政服务 _____   万国邮联 _____

国际邮政通信 _____	国际邮政法规 _____
双边协定 _____	邮政经营理事会 _____
重量单位 _____	邮政行业 _____
运输方式 _____	直复营销商 _____
水陆路邮件 _____	航空邮件 _____

 The World Postal Network: Reaching Everyone Everywhere.
— UPU

Unit 2 Post Office

Lead in

 Look at the picture first, then watch the video and discuss the following questions.

1. What services are offered at the Swiss virtual post office?
2. What services can you get from a post office in China according to your experience?

Audio-Visual

 Watch the video and answer the following questions.

1. What is the office hour of a Packstation every day?
2. Why does Deutsche Post send customers' welcome package and gold card by registered mail?
3. How do customers choose their preferred Packstation to send their parcels?

4. How does a customer make payment at a Packstation?

5. What are the other ways to send parcels from a Packstation?

3 Watch the video again and fill out the blanks with what you hear.

Registration

Registering for the Packstation service is (1) _____, either on line at *www.packstation.de*, by postcard or telephone. The customer receives his (2) _____ package along with his gold card just a few days after registration. For (3) _____ reasons, these are sent by registered mail along with the personal (4)_____ PostPIN number.

Ordering

Whether ordering from mail order(5) _____ or from the Internet, all you have to do is enter the number of your preferred Packstation as the (6) _____. You can also send parcels yourself to any Packstation. DHL, Deutsche Post Worldnet Parcel Express (7)_____ service will deliver to the Packstation of your choice. And there is almost always one close by.

 Reading 1

4 Read the passage below. Choose the best title for each numbered paragraph.

A Home Delivery Service
B Partner Service
C Mobile Post Office
D Hosted Service
E Private Service

Post Office® of the Royal Mail

Post Office Ltd is a wholly owned subsidiary of Royal Mail Group. (1) <u>With a nationwide network of Post Office® branches across the country the Post Office® network is the UK's biggest retailer.</u> The history of Post Office® dates back to 1635 when Charles I opened up his private mail service to the general public.

Vocabulary Assistant

subsidiary *n*. 子公司，分公司

Post Office® branches were established originally for the acceptance of mail, but their use expanded to include the payment of pensions and other financial transactions. Post Office® now offers more than 170 different products and services, including telephony, financial services, letters & parcels, insurance and travel related products. Post Office Ltd is now the largest provider of foreign currency in the UK and the leading independent provider of travel insurance.

Post Office® services are provided online and by phone in addition to face to face. There are lots of different types of outlets in our network, including Crown Office branches in city centres, outlets run by subpostmasters that combine a shop with the Post Office® branch, as well as outreach services including mobile Post Offices®, and services that visit village halls or churches.

Outreach services are an innovative way to provide customers with access to Post Office® products and services in communities where a traditional Post Office® is not practical. For the majority of outreach services, an established subpostmaster (known as the "core" subpostmaster) will travel to, or oversee service at, a nearby community to provide a local Post Office® service in addition to running their own Post Office® branch. (2) This enables Post Office Ltd to maintain a service in smaller communities in addition to supporting existing branches.

1. _____

A mobile Post Office® is a modern, fully equipped van offering Post Office® services. There are more than 168 villages currently visited by a mobile branch across the UK today. These communities are visited at set times and days each week, and the majority of Post Office® products and services are available through the Mobile service. These vehicles have an access lift at the back to assist elderly or disabled customers.

2. _____

The hosted service is operated from a local community building such as a cafe, village hall or community centre at set times and days each week, with space set aside at these premises for the portable Post Office® computer equipment. This enables customers to access the majority of Post Office® products and services at these locations.

Vocabulary Assistant

establish v. 建立，设立
insurance n. 保险
subpostmaster n. 代办英国邮政业务的商店店主
oversee v. 监督，指导
van n. 厢式货车
portable adj. 便携式的，手提的

telephony n. 电话业务
outlet n. 营业网点
community n. 社区
maintain v. 保持，维持
majority n. 多数，大半
location n. 地点，场所

3. _____

The partner service is combined in an existing retail premises and the local partner (such as the shop-owner), provides a slightly reduced range of Post Office® products and services from their premises. (3) <u>More than 80% of the full range of Post Office® products and services are available through the partner service and services are generally available during the same opening hours as the partner's retail business.</u>

4. _____

This is a service for very small communities and enables customers to order a reduced range of Post Office® products and services over the telephone. The products may either be delivered to a customer's home by the core subpostmaster or are available for collection by the customer at a local Drop-In Session.

Post Office Ltd serves over 21.2 million customers a week who make 31 million visits and approximately 47 million transactions. Approximately 92% of the UK adult population visit a Post Office® branch each year.

> **Vocabulary Assistant**
>
> premises *n.* 生产经营场所
> transaction *n.* 交易，业务
> approximately *adv.* 大约，几乎

5 *Read the above passage again, and translate the underlined sentences into Chinese.*

1. _____
2. _____
3. _____

6 *Complete the sentences with the proper form of the word given in the brackets.*

1. If you want to work in a post office, you must learn some mail- _____ (relation) words.
2. The British government today set out details of its plan to create a Post Office Bank _____ (offer) new financial services locally.
3. EMS can be sent from post office counters or it can be collected from customers' _____ (premise).
4. There is always a special entrance to every post office for the _____ (able).
5. In UK, Post Office® is actually one of the biggest _____ (retail).
6. Our customer service is _____ (avail) by telephone, short message or at the website.

Reading 2

7 Read the numbered paragraphs of *Being Your Own Postman*. Which paragraph does each of the following sentences refer to?

A   The APCs open every day in a year.
B   With credit cards, customers can buy insurances through APCs.
C   The services at post offices are limited by the closing time.
D   There are limits for the packages accepted by the parcel slot.
E   One can use credit cards at the APCs.

Being Your Own Postman

Automated Postal Center Makes Mailing Quicker, Easier, More Convenient

Waiting in line at the post office to buy stamps or send a package may be one of the most disliked chores of the holiday season. Now you can say goodbye to long lines at the post office and hello to quick service at your fingertips. With Post Office's new Automated Postal Center (APC), you can weigh your packages, dispense postage and send your mail on its way—all by yourself.

You no longer need a clerk to withdraw money from the bank, check out groceries at the supermarket or fuel up at the gas station. Now add the post office to the list of places where you can wait on yourself.

1   "We close at 7 p.m. on weekdays, but now that doesn't matter," said Postmaster Lou DiPerna. "The APC is in the lobby and can be accessed at any time, which is especially nice during the holidays."

2   APCs are self-service kiosks that accept credit or debit cards and perform the majority of postal transactions. They are open 24 hours a day, seven days a week and 365 days a year.

Vocabulary Assistant

chore *n.* 家务事，杂事
dispense *v.* 分配，派发
grocery *n.* 食品，杂货

fingertip *n.* 指尖
withdraw *v.* 提款
kiosk *n.* 售货亭，亭子

3 Using credit or debit cards, customers can use an APC to:
- Purchase self-adhesive stamps.
- Weigh, calculate and purchase postage in any amount for items weighing up to 70 lbs.
- Send items via Express Mail, Priority Mail, First-Class Mail and Parcel Post Services.
- Look up ZIP Codes and obtain mailing information.
- Obtain Express Mail, Certified Mail, and Return Receipts.
- Purchase Delivery Confirmation Service.
- Purchase Insurance ($200 maximum).
- Obtain a receipt.
- APCs are located next to a convenient parcel slot that accepts packages up to 12"H× 14"D×20"W.

The whole goal behind APCs is to provide the customer with a convenient, self-service alternative to the full-service counter. The machines are situated in larger offices where they have the most walk-in traffic.

In every post office lobby where an APC is installed, there has initially been an APC host—a USPS worker—greeting customers, encouraging them to try the self-serve kiosks and in many cases walking them through the steps. A touch screen on the kiosk prompts users in what to do next. Once customers have applied the postage sticker to their envelope or package, they open the slot and drop in the mailed piece.

Vocabulary Assistant

purchase *v.* 购买
maximum *n.* 最大限度，最大量
alternative *n.* 抉择，可供选择的办法
prompt *v.* 提示；鼓励

adhesive *adj.* 带粘性的
receipt *n.* 收据
install *v.* 安装，安置
sticker *n.* 涂有粘胶的标签或纸片

8 *Pay attention to the italicized parts in the English sentences and translate the Chinese sentences by simulating the structure of the English sentences.*

1. The whole *goal* behind APCs is to *provide* the customer *with* a convenient, self-service alternative to the full-service counter.
   我们的目标是向顾客提供优质的服务。

2. There has initially been an APC host—a USPS worker—greeting customers, encouraging them to try the self-serve kiosks and in many cases *walking* them *through* the steps.

这是一场关于指导客户了解投诉程序的会议。

_____

3. The APC is in the lobby and can *be accessed* at any time, which is especially nice during the holidays.

   这两种服务都可以从网站的链接上找到。

   _____

4. Once customers have *applied* the postage sticker *to* their envelope or package, they open the slot and drop in the mailed piece.

   你最好是在两面都涂上胶水。

   _____

9 **Complete the sentences with the following words, changing the form if necessary.**

| alternative | withdraw | via | install | confirmation | prompt |

1. A map will appear which _____ you for certain information.
2. Electronic invoice and remittance is provided to you _____ computer transmission.
3. Recent initiatives include _____ a new truck wash system that recycles water and rainwater tanks to provide water for gardens at certain mail centres.
4. Call 1-800-399-5999 to _____ if we serve your city.
5. If you are sending a gift, our gift bags are a great _____.
6. The counter cash _____ service is available in all post office branches.

Extended Practice

10 **The following are some things used in the post office. Please put each of them in the proper positions below its picture.**

| bubble | packing tape | envelope | packing box | mail tube |
| label | mail sticker | scale | cushion envelope | |

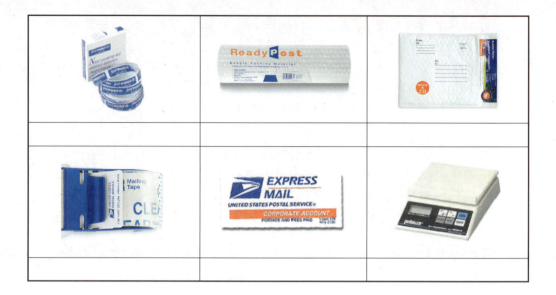

Professional Skills

11 *The following are short dialogues taking place in the post office. Use them and Postal Service Daily English provided in Unit 1 to make a COMPLETE conversation about mailing international letters with your partner.*

交寄国际信函 (Mailing International Letters)

1. 邮寄方式 (Ways of Mailing)

   Customer: I want to mail these letters to Italy.
   Clerk: By airmail?
   Customer: Yes.
   Clerk: Would you like them registered?
   Customer: No.

2. 收取费用 (Charging the Mail)

   Customer: How much, please?
   Clerk: Your total comes to 120 yuan.
   Customer: Here's 200 yuan.
   Clerk: Thank you. Here is your change. Anything else?
   Customer: No, thank you.
   Clerk: You're welcome.

POST OFFICE UNIT 2   21

交寄国际挂号信函 (Mailing Registered Letters)

Customer: I'd like to mail a letter to Canada.

Clerk: By registered mail?

Customer: Yes.

Clerk: Please write down your name and your complete address in case of non-delivery.

12 **Address the envelope properly with the two addresses below in correct order.**

Sender: P. R. CHINA
            DADONG DISTRICT
            SHENYANG, LIAONING 110044
            SHENYANG FINE CHEMICAL GENERAL FACTORY
            8-7 GUANQUAN ROAD

Receiver: PO Box 61625
             Admissions Office
             London SE9 2XY
             University of Greenwich
             UK
             Southwood Site

①
_____
_____
_____
_____

②
_____
_____
_____
_____

13 *Number the names of the countries according to the map, and translate them into Chinese.*

Europe

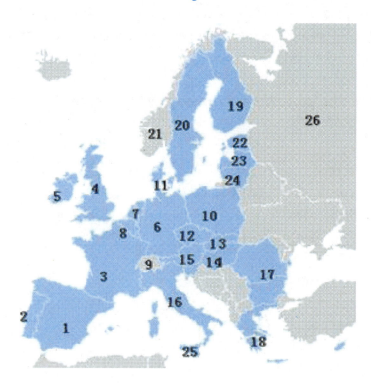

Example:
(4) United Kingdom _____英国_____   (16) Italy _____意大利_____

( ) Russia _____   ( ) Lithuania _____
( ) Czech _____   ( ) Latvia _____
( ) Malta _____   ( ) Poland _____
( ) Ireland _____   ( ) Slovakia _____
( ) Denmark _____   ( ) Sweden _____
( ) Belgium _____   ( ) Austria _____
( ) Finland _____   ( ) Estonia _____
( ) Switzerland _____   ( ) Norway _____
( ) Spain _____   ( ) Portugal _____
( ) Germany _____   ( ) Greece _____
( ) France _____   ( ) Hungary _____
( ) the Netherlands _____   ( ) Romania _____

Get to Know the Post

The logo of China Post combines the calligraphy of Chinese character "中" with the image of the postal network. The shape of wings implies message exchange or "Hong Yan Chuan Shu" — an old saying in China.

Simple but vigorous, the logo is mainly made up of horizontal and vertical parallels, indicating the sense of order and far reaches. The right-leaning writing gives the sense of direction and speed.

The logo indicates the target of China Post which is to serve thousands of households and its image which is to be rapid, accurate, safe and far reaching. The green color, which was decided by the first National Postal Conference in December 1949, symbolizes peace, youth, flourish and prosperity.

Logo of China Post

However, in ancient China, the logo of the Post had red as its main color. According to ancient documents in Han dynasty, the messengers were dressed in red and wore red scarves. The color of mail bags were a combination of red and white. This

was to let the carriages and pedestrians along the road easily recognize messengers coming from a long distance away, and make way for them to speed up the delivery.

 ## Do It Yourself

Find the English equivalents of the following Chinese from this unit.

Notebook

英国皇家邮政集团 _____   养老金支付业务 _____

UNIT 2 POST OFFICE

金融服务	_____	外汇	_____
旅游保险	_____	流动邮局	_____
延伸服务	_____	合作服务	_____
托管服务	_____	上门投递业务	_____
自动邮寄中心	_____	信用卡	_____
借记卡	_____	速递邮件	_____
优先邮件	_____	一类邮件	_____
包裹业务	_____	邮政编码	_____
投递确认业务	_____	回执	_____
美国邮政	_____	国际信函	_____
航空邮件	_____	挂号邮件	_____

 As a modern post, our people are the heart and soul of our company.
— Canada Post

Unit 3 Mail Carrier

Lead in

1 Watch the video and answer the following questions.

1. What characteristics should a rural carrier have?
2. Why do you think a rural carrier's job is very important to the farmers?
3. The rural carrier said "We mean a lot to the people. They mean a lot to us." Do you agree and why?
4. What are the differences between a rural carrier and a city carrier?

Audio-Visual

2 Watch the video and answer the following questions.

1. Who is Aaron?
2. How many mail items are delivered daily in New Zealand?
3. What types of posties are mentioned in this video?
4. How long does a postie usually work a day?
5. What are the qualifications for the job of a postie?

3 Watch the video again and fill out the blanks with what you hear.

New Zealand posties generally start the day as a team (1 where) _____, spending 2-3 hours (2 doing what) _____ for delivery. There may be team meetings (3 when) _____, where posties brief important information around (4 what) _____. Before going to deliver the mail, posties take a rest to refuel and hydrate their body. Then they make a safety check on (5 what) _____. Unless it's unsafe, the mail is delivered in all types of weather, as safety is their (6 what) _____.

Reading 1

4 The following key phrases describe Jeannette Bell's whole day work. Put them in right order according to the passage.

① deliver her letters
② sort the magazines and packets
③ sort her letter mails
④ takes her gear back
⑤ add redirection sticker with new address
⑥ load her bike

Delivering the Mail

Over 2000 New Zealand Post Posties deliver mail to over 1.5 million home and business addresses around the country, mostly six days a week. A team of Rural Post people deliver mail to rural and outlying areas. Mail is also delivered to businesses and private boxes.

Most Posties first sort the mail at their Local Delivery Branch, starting work early in the morning. Their day is usually around six hours. Posties deliver addressed letters, advertising circulars, packets and 'large flats' (large envelopes).

A day in the life of a Postie

Jeannette Bell is a Postie in Palmerston North. Her round covers the city centre, with shops, businesses and a few houses. She works every day except Sunday.

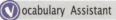

Vocabulary Assistant

outlying *adj.* 边远的，偏远的
circular *n.* 印制的广告，传单
sort *v.* 分拣，把……分类
packet *n.* 小包

7:00am

Jeannette arrives for work at the Manawatu Mail Centre in Palmerston North. (1) She begins sorting her letter mail into houses and shops, putting the private box mail to one side in number order. This will be sorted at the PostShop and put in private boxes.

8:00am

Jeannette puts rubber bands around letters to make bundles she can hold. Usually there are 20-25 bundles.

8:30am

She sorts the magazines and packets, bundling them up with rubber bands.

9:00am

Jeannette checks letters with no numbers or wrong numbers to see if she can work out the correct addresses. (2) If people have moved she adds a redirection sticker with the new address, and sends the mail on to them.

9:15am

Sorting is complete — she's ready to go! Jeannette puts the private box mail and big packets together, for the van driver to pick up. She puts on her helmet, and a jacket and gloves if it's cold or wet. Then she loads her bike and heads out the door.

9:30am

Jeannette cycles along, delivering to letterboxes and getting off her bike to go into businesses. She has to watch out for cars backing out of driveways.

11:00am

Her bike round is finished. She's covered 15 kilometres. At the PostShop, Jeannette stops for a short morning tea break.

11:15am

She's off again. This time she's on foot, with her walking bag. Her eight kilometre route takes her around the shops and malls delivering mail to counters. Sometimes she takes a lift or walks up the stairs to deliver to customers. Along her route, customers often ask questions about postage and parcels, and people on the street ask her for directions.

Vocabulary Assistant

Manawatu 马纳瓦图（新西兰城市名） Palmerston North 北帕默斯顿（新西兰城市名）
bundle n. 信把 redirection n. 改寄
sticker n. 粘贴标签 helmet n. 头盔
load v. 装 head v. 朝着……去
driveway n. 车道 watch out (for) 提防，密切注意
back out (of) 倒出

1:15pm

All the mail is delivered. The mail bags are empty. Jeannette takes her gear back to the Delivery Branch — she has finished for the day.

Delivering the Mail — Rural Areas

People who live in rural areas or on the outskirts of a town have mail delivered to their gate by Rural Post. It would be too hard for a Postie to get to these areas.

Rural Post people mostly use cars and vans. Sometimes they use buses, trucks and even boats. (3) <u>As well as delivering, they collect mail and CourierPost items from customers' Rural Post letterboxes, which open at the front.</u>

Customers can buy stamps and other products such as envelopes and HandiBags from Rural Post drivers. Drivers also deliver newspapers, advertising circulars and even bread and milk for customers who live in remote areas.

Rural Post people are independent contractors. The service is free to customers.

(4) <u>Rural Post letterboxes all have a front flap which the Rural Post driver can open from their vehicle.</u> On the side of the box is a flag. When a customer has mail for collection, they put it in the letterbox and raise the flag. The driver sees the flag and stops to pick up the mail.

Vocabulary Assistant

gear n.（某种活动的）装备，用具　　outskirts n. 郊外
contractor n. 承包人　　flap n. 门扇，封盖

5 Read the above passage again, and translate the underlined sentences into Chinese.

1. _____

2. _____

3. _____

4. _____

6 Complete the sentences with the following words, changing the form if necessary.

deliver   pick up   sticker   sort   bundle   collect

1. If you are required to _____ your mail _____ at the post office, you need to find the correct location and the appropriate service counter when you arrive.
2. The housewife writes that every morning the postman opens her gate and undoes his _____ of letters and then drops his rubber bands outside her front door.
3. On Saturday, there will be no delivery to street addresses, no scheduled _____ of mail from blue collection boxes or pickup of mail from homes and businesses.
4. Please fill out this green label and Customs Declaration, then _____ the green label to your packet.
5. You can request proof of _____ to be emailed, faxed, or mailed to you for no additional fee for Express Mail and Signature Confirmation services.
6. The next generation of barcode technology used to _____ and track mail will be exhibited at the mailing industry's leading trade show, National Postal Forum.

Reading 2

7 Read the passage below. Choose the best title for each numbered story. Write the corresponding title on the line before each story.

A Eye on the Elderly
B Help on the Way
C Fire and Rescue
D Neighbourhood Watch
E Animal Action

> Messenger of Sympathy and Love
> Servant of Parted Friends
> Consoler of the Lonely
> Bond of the Scattered Family
> Enlarger of the Common Life
> Carrier of News and Knowledge
> Instrument of Trade and Industry
> Promoter of Mutual Acquaintance
> Of Peace and of Goodwill Among Men and Nations

Proud to Serve
NATIONAL ASSOCIATION OF LETTER CARRIERS

In this modern age, with greed and violence staples in the news, examples of courage and compassion are more important than ever. Across the US, letter carriers are often the first to discover people in need due to accidents, attacks or fires. The following reports are offered to honor the actions of all NALC members whose quick thinking and sharp reactions have saved lives.

1 _____

Maria Elena Romero noticed the flag up on a curbside mailbox, so she reached out

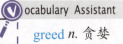

greed n. 贪婪
staple n. 主题，主要内容
curbside n. 路边
violence n. 暴力
compassion n. 同情心

to grab the mail. In the stack were a few outgoing letters, but on top was a note addressed "Mailperson." The note began, "Call 911. I'm dead. I am in the bathroom and I left all doors open. Please find a nice home for my two cats," which the note described. Romero knew the woman and knew this letter was no joke. She decided not to enter the home, instead grabbing her cell phone to call 911 and then call her supervisor. A police officer soon arrived, read the note, checked the doors (all unlocked) and peered through the windows. He saw two cats that matched the descriptions. The officer called for assistance and told Romero to remain on the scene. The customer was found in the bathroom with a blanket wrapped around her, unconscious but still alive. Paramedics soon arrived and, suspecting that she overdosed on medication, rushed her to a hospital. After being interviewed by police, the Fresno, California Branch 231 member resumed her route. Romero was credited with saving her customer's life. "I don't believe I need recognition," she said. "I just did what I felt was right."

2 _____

JOSEPH ASHLEY to the house of Sandra Leicht, a patron he knew well. Because she has limited mobility, her mailbox was installed right by her door so she could just reach out and grab her mail. Or, if the door was open and she was nearby, the carrier would enter and hand-deliver the mail. This day, however, something was wrong — Ashley saw Leicht apparently unconscious while she was baby-sitting her 4-year-old great-granddaughter. When Leicht didn't respond to Ashley's calls at the door, he quickly called 911 and summoned an ambulance. The Muncie, Indiana Branch 98 member stayed with his patron until paramedics arrived. It was determined the customer had passed out due to low blood sugar. Once Ashley finished his route, he came back to check on the woman. "Bless his heart," Leicht told the Star Press. "If it

---

Vocabulary Assistant

grab v. 抓取
outgoing adj. 发出的，外寄的
peer v. 仔细看，端详
unconscious adj. 失去知觉的，未觉察到的
overdose v. 一次用药过量
Fresno 弗雷斯诺（美国加利福尼亚州中西部城市）
California 加利福尼亚州（美国州名）
credit v. 认为是……功劳，把……归于
patron n. 顾客
reach out 伸出（手）
summon v. 召集
Indiana 印第安纳州（美国州名）
low blood sugar 低血糖

stack n. 堆，垛
supervisor n. 监管人
on the scene 现场
paramedic n. 护理人员
medication n. 药物
resume v. 重返，继续
recognition n. 赞誉，承认
mobility n. 活动
babysit v. 照看
Muncie 曼西（美国印第安纳州城市）
pass out 昏迷，昏厥
the Star Press 曼西星空通讯社

hadn't been for him, I don't know what would have happened."

3 _____

Seeing a toddler clutching her blanket and stepping out into the street right where it curves, Ed Markowitz quickly took action. The 25-year postal veteran stopped oncoming traffic and walked the child back to safety. The girl was too young to tell the carrier where she lived and Markowitz saw no adults. Recruiting a customer he knew well to watch the child, the carrier began knocking on doors of homes where he was aware children lived. He was having no luck until he came to a house where the door was answered by two children, both under 10 years old. Their guilt was evident when they realized their little sister had slipped away. The father was shocked when he was roused with the news and expressed his gratitude to the Pueblo, Colorado Branch 229 member upon his child's return. Markowitz returned to his rounds without reporting the incident. The act only came to light when a postal customer who had witnessed the event brought it to the attention of the postmaster.

Vocabulary Assistant

toddler *n.* 学步的儿童
curve *v.* 绕弯，成曲线
veteran *n.* 老手，富有经验的人
recruit *v.* 动员（提供帮助）
rouse *v.* 唤醒
slip away 溜走
witness *v.* 目击，见证

clutch *v.* 抱住，抓住
take action 采取行动
oncoming *adj.* 迎面而来的
guilt *n.* 内疚
Pueblo 普韦布洛（美国科罗拉多州城市）
Colorado 科罗拉多州（美国州名）

8 **Complete the sentences with the following words, changing the form if necessary.**

> supervisor   witness   credit   unconscious   peer   compassion

1. As an old postman who has been with post for more than thirty years, he _____ every important development in postal technology.
2. NALC celebrated six courageous and _____ carriers as its 2009 National Heroes of the Year.
3. Jack Lee, the mail carrier, was _____ by the Police Department with saving the woman's life.
4. Posties gain their skills on the job, usually with _____ from experienced members of staff.
5. The new postman _____ through the mist, trying to find the right house.
6. When the letter carrier found the old lady faint, he prevented her from collapsing and quickly brought her back to _____.

9 **Pay attention to the italicized parts in the English sentences and translate the Chinese sentences by simulating the structure of the English sentences.**

1. Across this nation, letter carriers are often *the first to* discover people in need due to accidents, attacks or fires.
   在邮件处理中心，操作人员常常是第一个报告邮件以及设备问题的人。

2. She *decided not to* enter the home, *instead* grabbing her cell phone to call 911 and then call her supervisor.
   她决定不亲自去售票处买票，而是拨打11185客服热线订票。

3. *If it hadn't been for* him, I don't know what would have happened.
   要不是因为邮递员的勇敢，那位老人早已经在大火中丧生了。

4. The act *only came to light when* a postal customer who had witnessed the event brought it to the attention of the postmaster.
   当顾客通知当地电视台后，这个邮递员的行为才被人知晓。

Extended Practice

10 **The following are some pictures of delivery vehicles. Give the name of the country each belongs to.**

post bike

delivery trolley

cargo tricycle

post motorcycle

electric cycle with trailer

delivery cart

11 The following are pictures of different postboxes. Give the name of the country each belongs to.

mail slot

mail box

cluster box

wall box

pillar box

letter box

12 The following postcard is made by Australia Post to educate customers on how to keep the posties safe on their beat. Look at the postcard and discuss the following questions.

1. As a customer, where and how do you think the letterbox should be installed in order to make it easier and safer for your postie to deliver the mail?
2. Besides improperly installed letterbox, what else may cause danger to your postie?

Professional Skills

13 **The following are short dialogues taking place in the post office. Use them and Postal Service Daily English provided in Unit 1 to make a COMPLETE conversation about mailing postcards with your partner.**

交寄明信片 (Mailing Postcards)

1. 贴邮票 (Sticking Stamps)

   Clerk: Please stick the stamp on the upper right-hand corner, and then drop it into the mailbox.

   Customer: Can I stick stamps on the back of the card?

   Clerk: I'm afraid you cannot. Stamps must be put on the front of cards.

2. 邮资明信片 (Prepaid Postcards)

   Customer: I want to mail these postcards to Britain.

   Clerk: These are domestic prepaid postcards. I'm afraid that you have to put 3.7 yuan stamps on each of them.

14 **Address the envelope properly with the two addresses below in correct order.**

Sender: NO 4, FOURTH LOK YANG RD
SINGAPORE 629701
DANONE MARKETING (SINGAPORE) PTE LTD
LI MING

Receiver: USA
Seattle, WA 98112
Zhang Tao
USPS #98112
1463 E. Republican St.

15 Number the names of the countries according to the map, and translate them into Chinese.

North America

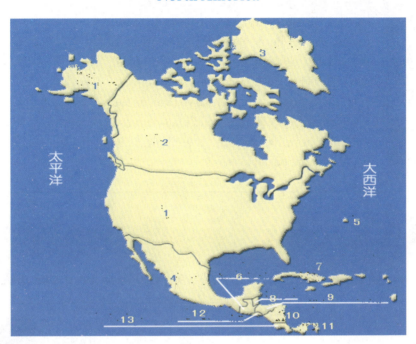

Example:
(1) United States of America _____美国_____   (2) Canada _____加拿大_____

( ) Panama _____   ( ) Honduras _____
( ) Bermuda _____   ( ) Cuba _____
( ) Belize _____   ( ) Guatemala _____
( ) Greenland _____   ( ) Costa Rica _____
( ) Mexico _____   ( ) El Salvador _____
( ) Nicaragua _____

Get to Know the Post

In early 17th century, some European countries had prosperous butcher activities. Animal dealers used horns to signal their buying animals. They had great mobility and specific routes, therefore, the postal administration entrusted them with a task of collecting and delivering mails at a very

low price. Whenever people heard the sound of the horns, they knew they could send mails. Later on, animal trade gradually became waned, animal dealers were no longer engaged in long-distance trades, but the horn was kept and evolved to the symbol of mail messengers and postal carriages. Thus, in Europe, the horn is closely related to post even in today. Due to the relationship between horns and mail-delivery, this post horn has become the emblem for many national postal systems.

Post Horn

 Do It Yourself

Find the English equivalents of the following Chinese from this unit.

Notebook

分拣邮件	_____	投递局	_____
投递邮件	_____	邮袋	_____
企业信箱	_____	揽收邮件	_____
私人信箱	_____	邮递员	_____
扁平函件	_____	邮（信）筒	_____
右上角	_____	橡皮筋	_____
国内邮资明信片	_____	邮政商店	_____
全国邮递员协会	_____	信封	_____

 On land and online, we deliver.

— Canada Post

Unit 4 Customer Service

Lead in

1 **Discuss the following questions according to the pictures given below.**

1. What qualities should the call center staff possess?
2. Does the facial expression of the call center staff matter and in what way?
3. What services does China Post Customer Service Center provide?

Audio-Visual

2 **Watch the video and answer the following questions.**

1. Besides efficiency, what other qualities of the postmen are regarded as important by postal customers?
2. How does Mrs. Rigby describe the appearance of today's postmen?

3. Despite the complaints, some customers are still happy with their postmen. For what reasons?

4. Why does one of the customers want to give the postman a brush?

3 **Watch the video again and fill out the blanks with what you hear.**

"He was clean and smart and had an air of (1) _____ about him. He was also very (2) _____. During the time it took me to get to the front door, the postman didn't bang (3) _____ at the door, nor did he ring the bell again. I would like him to know that his bearing and (4) _____ is much (5) _____. And I hope he will let no one (6) _____ him from any standards he has set for himself."

Mrs. Archer writes her corner house is the first in the road to which a postman delivers. "Every morning he opens my gate and (7) _____ his bundle of letters and then drop his (8) _____ bands outside my front door. My dog nearly choked on one yesterday. Perhaps you could ask your postmen to be more careful in future."

Reading 1

4 **Read the numbered principles. Match each of the following sentences with one principle.**

A Customers may feel satisfied when they are warmly served.
B Nobody likes being ignored.
C The post company can benefit from selling additional service to customers.
D Postal employees are irreplaceable in selling proper services to customers.
E The postal employees are encouraged to accept complaints and handle them actively.

How to Treat Your Customers?

Treat your customers as you would like to be treated yourself. This is the golden service rule for all postal employees. To achieve this rule, you must know what your customers are looking for and possess the necessary professional morality.

1. Your customers are looking for far more than just stamps.

What they need is your:

Assistance, Advice and Information.

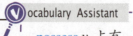

Vocabulary Assistant

possess v. 占有，拥有　　professional adj. 专业的
morality n. 道德；伦理　　far more than 远不只是

If you give these things freely, accurately and with a smile, your customers will go away content with your service. If your service is outstanding they will come back. If your service is bad they will most likely go elsewhere.

Remember that many customers:

    Don't say much.

    Don't complain.

    Don't come back.

2. Don't just take the money and run. Something is MORE IMPORTANT than price!

What your customers are really looking for is:

    Reliability and Good Service.

Remember your customers are hungry for good service and they are prepared to pay for it. They will forgive a mistake, but they will NEVER forgive a bad attitude. The good service is up to you.

3. Talking to people makes:

    Your day go faster and your work more interesting.

Machines can supply stamps in exchange for money. Only you, real people, can SELL the right service to your customers.

4. Remember that in every job there are two parts:

    Rules and People.

You can all learn the rules of your job but you must realize that your customers are people and therefore you should treat them accordingly. If you can master both areas, you will love any job you undertake. To be able to achieve this you must:

    Pay attention.

    Realize people like being noticed, not just shuffled through.

    Look them in the eye.

    Give them that "Personal Touch"

Treat your customers as individuals and they will treat you as individuals. Your customers will remember you if you remember them.

5. When serving your customers you should realize that:

    You're here to help.

    You shouldn't treat people like numbers.

    You should use their names.

    You should ask questions.

By asking questions you can show that you're interested in solving their problems. Be

Vocabulary Assistant

accurately *adv.* 精确地
outstanding *adj.* 杰出的
reliability *n.* 可靠性
accordingly *adv.* 相应地

content *adj.* 心满意足的
complain *v.* 抱怨
in exchange for 作为……的交换
individual *n.* 个人

genuinely concerned and show sympathy and understanding of their feelings.

6. Your customer may not be aware of all your services. By asking the right questions, you can suggest extra services. When a customer buys an extra service then you have three winners:

    Customer, Post and You.

7. If you welcome complaints you're able to rectify the problem, then you are contributing towards your Striving for Excellence.

8. You should also realize that sometimes for no apparent reason your customers may feel:

    Hassled, Upset, Angry and Confused.

So you should always think about your customers' feelings. For example, if you must leave them at the counter to go away and gain the information you need, tell them what you are doing and why. Don't leave them guessing. One person's attitude towards a customer can change that customer's opinion of the whole organization. Keep your customers satisfied. Dissatisfaction leads to losing customers and losing customers means less revenue.

9. Finally by asking questions you are able to find out the customers' true needs and not your perceived idea of these needs. Once you have found out their needs then you are able to make suggestions that will help them to gain the service best suited to them. Remember the customer does not like waiting, especially when it is not necessary. You know that sometimes long queues make it impractical to give your customers anything other than fast service, but fast service with a smile can send them away happy.

As a bare minimum, you must always smile, greet your customers and say "Thank you".

Vocabulary Assistant

genuinely *adv.* 真正地
rectify *v.* 纠正；改正
hassle *v.* 打扰，麻烦
perceive *v.* 感知
be aware of 意识到

sympathy *n.* 同情
apparent *adj.* 明显的
revenue *n.* 收入，收益
bare *adj.* 仅有的

5 *Pay attention to the italicized parts in the English sentences and translate the Chinese sentences by simulating the structure of the English sentences.*

1. You must realize that your customers are people and therefore you should treat them *accordingly*.

   作为邮政营业员，你应当充分了解客户的问题，然后根据情况进行处理。

2. Remember your customers *are hungry for* good service and they *are prepared to* pay for it.

   她非常渴望成功，甚至愿意为此付出任何代价。

3. Your customer may not *be aware of* all your services.
   邮政员工都很了解中国邮政的环保政策及其积极影响。

4. Your customers are looking for *far more than just* stamps.
   现代化的邮局提供的服务远不仅仅是邮寄信函和包裹。

6 Complete the sentences with the following words, changing the form if necessary.

| professional | sympathy | reliability | rectify | complain | apparent |

1. This program helps postal _____ gain skills to successfully manage mail centers.
2. The company is in a bad situation and _____ it is losing a lot of money.
3. A written _____ may be submitted by an individual or company to the related department.
4. On behalf of my family, I _____ with those who lost their loved ones in this accident.
5. The Postal Service's mission is to provide the nation with _____, affordable, universal mail service.
6. _____ wrong addresses is required by the post to reduce non-delivery rates.

Reading 2

7 Read the passage below. Choose the best title for each numbered paragraph.

A Calm the customer by questioning.
B Focus the customer on the problem.
C Handling customer complaints.
D Maintain a friendly and professional attitude.
E Keep the customers calm by smile.
F Acknowledge that a difficult situation exists.
G Handling the problem.

Dealing with Difficult Customers

A customer's anger is sometimes a common emotional response to a frustrating situation. As counter staff, you will have to deal with difficult customers from time

Vocabulary Assistant

emotional *adj.* 感情的   frustrating *adj.* 令人泄气的，使人沮丧的

to time.(1) <u>Occasionally it is enough to make you angry and upset as well.</u> When your customers lost their temper, remember it is important that you, as a professional, don't lose yours — STAY CALM. Dealing with difficult customers, you need to follow these steps:

1 _____

If the customer attacks you verbally, don't take it personally. The customer is probably angry at the situation, not YOU. Don't argue back. Use your communication skills to deal with the situation.

2 _____

When discussing the situation with the customer, use terms and a tone that shows sensitivity to the customer's feelings. Often when a customer is upset, it is not just because of the problem, he may be distressed about various sorts of things: cat and dog problems, health, family, rent, tax problems, etc. Be sure to show sympathy for what he is going through. By giving assurance and having a friendly manner, you can calm the frustration.

3 _____

By asking the customer pertinent questions, you show that you are giving attention to his problem. By verifying the problem/situation, you may also calm his frustrations. By questioning and verifying the situation, you're getting him to work with you to find a solution to his problem.

4 _____

Ask the customer questions to gain his assistance in focusing on his problem. Remember you are enlisting the customer's help to arrive at a solution to his problem. After you have — calmed the customer,
               — verified the problem and
               — focused on the problem,
Move onto Step 5.

5 _____

Solving the problem isn't easy sometimes. (2) <u>Be sure to explain to the customer what you intend to do, so that he understands the solution.</u> Remember difficult customers are just like anyone else, they want courteous, efficient service and special attention to their particular problem. You won't be able to solve everyone's problem, but by following these steps you can make sure you have done your best. By showing sympathy with the customer, while solving his problem you will show that you

Vocabulary Assistant

occasionally *adv.* 偶尔
acknowledge *v.* 承认
pertinent *adj.* 恰当的；相关的

verbally *adv.* 言语上；口头地
be distressed about 对……感到痛苦的
courteous *adj.* 有礼貌的，殷勤的

are a true professional. Remember — dealing with difficult customers calmly and professionally can turn them into happy customers.

6 _____

Everyday life is full of complaints. (3) <u>Sometimes we complain and sometimes we are on the receiving end.</u> Sometimes we just store it and hope that it will go away. It depends more on how a complaint is made *rather than* what it is about.

Remember: don't ignore the complaint,
　　　　　 don't store the complaint,
　　　　　 don't react *aggressively*,
　　　　　 don't lose your temper,
　　　　　 don't take complaints personally,
　　　　　 don't make promises you can't keep.

You should: listen carefully, remain *detached*, don't *take sides*.

(4) <u>If you are not sure, it's wiser to give the benefit of the doubt to the customer.</u> Deal with it if you have the *authority*. If not, *pass* it *on* only *to* the person who does have the authority. If the customer is *at fault*, get him to agree by being firm and polite. If the complaint is justified, apologize *on behalf of* the post.

Complaints can often highlight weaknesses, and help you Strive for Excellence. You cannot improve, unless people tell you where you are going wrong.

Vocabulary Assistant

rather than 而不是	aggressively *adv.* 盛气凌人地
detached *adj.* 不偏不倚的	take sides 偏袒
authority *n.* 当权者；权威	pass on to 传递
at fault 有错误，出毛病	on behalf of 代表

8 **Read the above passage again, and translate the underlined sentences into Chinese.**

1. _____
2. _____
3. _____
4. _____

9 **Complete the sentences with the following words, changing the form if necessary.**

　　authority　　courteous　　highlight　　pertinent　　acknowledge　　detach

1. Australia Post is widely _____ internationally as a leading postal business.
2. The USPS has _____ a commemorative postmark to be issued in Oregon to help all state residents celebrate 150 years of statehood.
3. The mail service is after all a public service and it _____ the importance of the postal security.
4. The manager raised several _____ questions before promising to solve the problem.
5. Our drivers are living examples of the values we practice every day — Excellence, _____, Integrity, Trustworthiness and Efficiency.
6. A qualified employee must be _____ when dealing with customers' complaints.

Extended Practice

10 **Make a phone call with your partner to complete the whole process of handling the enquiry of an EMS item.**

| You are working at 11183 Call Center of China Post in Shijiazhuang. The phone is ringing. | You have sent an EMS item to your friend but he hasn't received it yet. You are calling to make an inquiry. |

1. Pick up the phone.

2. Introduce yourself and say that you want to check your EMS item.

3. You ask about the date of sending.

4. Tell about the date of sending and the destination of the item.

5. You ask about the EMS number.

6. Offer the number and ask about possible reasons of delay.

7. Explain it's a peak season and tell him you're checking for him.

8. Complain that it might be late for your friend's birthday.

9. Calm the customer by telling him that information shows the item has arrived the destination office.

10. Thanks for help.

Professional Skills

11 **The following are short dialogues taking place in the post office. Use them and Postal Service Daily English provided in Unit 1 to make a complete conversation about mailing small packets with your partner.**

交寄小包 (Mailing Small Packets)

1. 出示内件 (Showing the Contents)
   Customer: I'm going to mail this bag as small packets.
   Clerk: Would you show me the contents, please?
   Customer: All right.
2. 填写单式 (Filling in the Forms)
   Clerk: Now please fill in these forms.
   Customer: Here you are.
   Clerk: I am sorry. Please write the name of the contents in detail here. Then mark your choice here with a cross. Thank you.

12 **Translate the receiver's address for correct delivery.**

Customer Relations
International Mail Centre
PO BOX 325
New Zealand

Zhang Xiaohui
1-1-201
56 Fanxi Road
Shijiazhuang, Hebei 050016
P. R. China

13 **Number the English names of the countries according to the map, and match them with the Chinese equivalents.**

South America

( ) Bolivia   A 圭亚那
( ) Venezuela   B 哥伦比亚
( ) Brazil   C 智利
( ) Uruguay   D 厄瓜多尔
( ) Peru   E 委内瑞拉
( ) Ecuador   F 苏里南
( ) Colombia   G 巴西
( ) Chile   H 秘鲁
( ) Suriname   I 玻利维亚
( ) Paraguay   J 乌拉圭
( ) Guyana   K 阿根廷
( ) Argentina   L 巴拉圭

Get to Know the Post

Universal postal service is aimed at "ensuring the provision of a good quality, affordable universal postal service, allowing effective communication between people around the world".

Whether it is a personal letter from a close friend, a birthday card from a grandparent, a book or other goods ordered via the Internet, a bank statement or a holiday brochure — delivered to a home or a post box address — the majority of the world's citizens enjoy the benefits of universal postal service. The hundreds of thousands of postal outlets worldwide further ensure that customers have easy access to a diverse choice of service. In many small villages, the post office is often the only business.

Earthquakes, hurricanes, snowstorms and human conflict regularly cause serious damage and displace millions of people. The postal service is usually one of the first public services back at work after a disaster has struck. With telephone lines down and roads blocked off, letter carriers are often seen walking through the ruins, trying to find the recipients of letters from worried relatives. The postal service is also often used to deliver money and goods in times of disaster.

Universal Postal Service

 ## Do It Yourself

Find the English equivalents of the following Chinese from this unit.

Notebook

优质服务准则 _____   搪塞 _____
邮政员工 _____   职业道德 _____
力争优质服务 _____   窗口营业员 _____

沟通技巧	_____	偏袒	_____
发脾气	_____	小包	_____
出示内件	_____	填写单式	_____

 Postal Service: The People's Love.

— **Korean Post**

Unit 5 Philately

Lead in

1 Watch the video and discuss why stamps were invented.

2 Look at the picture and talk about the whole process of stamp making.

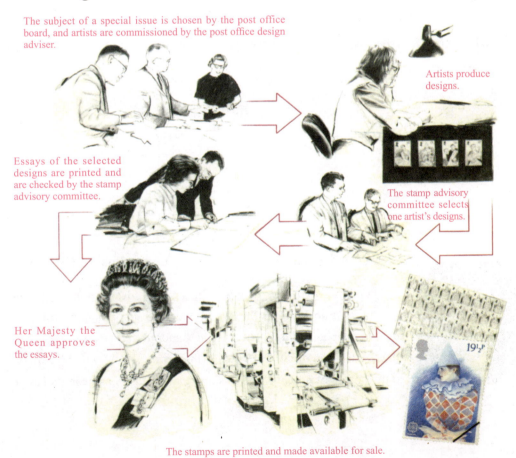

The subject of a special issue is chosen by the post office board, and artists are commissioned by the post office design adviser.

Artists produce designs.

Essays of the selected designs are printed and are checked by the stamp advisory committee.

The stamp advisory committee selects one artist's designs.

Her Majesty the Queen approves the essays.

The stamps are printed and made available for sale.

Audio-Visual

3 Watch the video and answer the following questions.

1. What was the great event in 1847?
2. What has made stamps become more exciting and appealing?

4 Watch the video again and fill out the blanks with what you hear.

For a long time, stamps stuck strictly to the "great man" theme, but in 1893 Postmaster General John Wannamaker started a (1) _____ of his own. He issued a series of stamps to (2) _____ the World's Fair, which was known as the Columbian Exposition. The Columbian Exposition stamps were a (3) _____; they told a story on the stamps. They told about the (4) _____ of America. Congress passed a joint (5) _____ calling these kind of images on stamps (6) _____. Despite congressional (7) _____, Wannamaker's gamble paid off. He proved that stamps could do much more than move mail. They could (8) _____ the public.

Reading 1

5 Fill in the following table according to the passage below.

The history of the postage stamp				
When	Who	Where	What ideas	What results
1840	Rowland Hill			
1848		Not mentioned		
1895	Not Mentioned			

Such a Simple Idea—The Story of the Postage Stamp

(1) It has often been said that the simplest ideas are the best. That is certainly true as far as the humble postage stamp is concerned. An idea developed in Great Britain one hundred and seventy years ago of a small piece of gummed paper (the Penny Black) which is affixed to the corner of an envelope to show that postage has been prepaid is

Vocabulary Assistant

humble *adj.* 不起眼的，粗陋的　　　gum *v.* 涂胶
prepaid *adj.* （邮资等）预先付讫的，已支付的

still in world-wide use today. Although the idea of the postage stamp spread quickly around the world, in the main, the size and shape of the postage stamp have remained unaltered.

People should not forget, however, that it was not only the concept of the postage stamp that emerged one hundred and seventy years ago. The stamp was linked with Sir Rowland Hill's proposals for a cheaper, uniform rate of postage which was paid by the sender rather than the recipient. The success of these schemes, and the enthusiasm with which they were greeted by the public led to their adoption throughout the world. It can be argued that the simple postage stamp gave rise to the birth of mass communication.

In those formative years, each stamp had to be removed from the large sheet using scissors. It was in 1848 that Henry Archer patented a system of inter-locking pins and holes, so that when the sheet of stamps was passed between the two, a series of holes was punched into the paper. Perforations had been born, thereby enabling stamps to be easily removed from the sheet.

In 1895, the first official stamp booklet was introduced in Luxembourg. Today customers can buy stamps in a convenient booklet form, not only from post office but from machines located outside post office building, so that they will always have some stamps ready to use. However, not all wished to buy a complete booklet in this way. Again, the idea of producing stamps in rolls developed in Great Britain.

Today communications are developing constantly, and many will question whether a mail system with postage stamps will be viable or indeed possible in the future. The fact remains that, despite the growth of electronic means of communication, more mail is being sent than ever before. (2) The public is realizing that a letter can be so much more personal, and needs a stamp. But the stamp has greatly exceeded its postal functions. Having become

Vocabulary Assistant

unaltered *adj.* 未被改变的，不变的，照旧的
scheme *n.* 方案，设计，办法
adoption *n.* 采用，采纳
mass *adj.* 大众的；大规模的，大量的
scissors *n.* 剪刀
punch *v.* 打孔
thereby *adv.* 因此，从而
viable *adj.* 可行的

uniform *adj.* 一样的，相同的
enthusiasm *n.* 热情，热心，积极性
argue *v.* 提出理由证明，表明
formative *adj.* 形成的
patent *v.* 取得……的专利权
perforation *n.* 齿孔
Luxembourg *n.* 卢森堡公国(西欧国家)

a highly coveted item, it has given rise to a science: philately. There are now countless collectors: large and small, people of all political persuasions and all social classes devote themselves to it, for pleasure, education and profit. As an ambassador of the issuing country, the postage stamp is assuredly a universal link among men—in more ways than one.

(3) One hundred and seventy years on the humble postage stamp is still very much with us. Perhaps the same may not be true in one hundred and seventy years time, but it will take a long time for the world to surrender this simple, British idea.

Vocabulary Assistant

covet v. 垂涎，羡慕
persuasion n. 信念，说服力，（持某一见解的）派别
devote oneself to 献身于，致力于
assuredly adv. 确实地，确信地
philately n. 集邮
ambassador n. 大使
surrender v. 放弃，使投降

Read the above passage again, and translate the underlined sentences into Chinese.

1. _____

2. _____

3. _____

6 Complete the sentences with the following words and phrases, changing the form if necessary.

| humble | uniform | patent | thereby | covet | give rise to |

1. For the UPU, the purpose of a new recasting of the Postal Payment Services Agreement would be to pave the way for the application of _____ principles.
2. The U.S. Postal Service commemorates the 200th anniversary of the birth of Abraham Lincoln, who rose from _____ origins to become a president.
3. Today, Posts should view their commitment to sustainable development and _____ satisfy their customers and improve their staff's living and working conditions.

4. The uncertainty of the market _____ extra cost in the postal enterprise.

5. It is illegal to sell or use a _____ invention without authorization of the _____ owner.

6. The stamp-collector finally got the souvenir folder he _____ for a long time by a mere accident.

Reading 2

7 Read the passage below, and choose from the following sentences the most suitable one to describe the main idea of each numbered paragraph.

A The word "philately" is from a non-English origin, and its meaning has changed greatly.
B Philatelists are a group of people deeply attracted by stamp collecting.
C The postage stamp has become the object of a hobby shortly after its invention.
D Philately enjoys a worldwide popularity.
E Philately is not only an activity of commerce but also a scholarly subject.

The Philatelist's Passion

1 The postage stamp was originally intended for prepaying the mail and it can be taken that its inventor, Sir Rowland Hill, did not in 1840 imagine that these labels would quickly become coveted objects for collectors and that this would give birth to a passion: philately. That passion was born almost immediately, as early as 1841, when a British woman placed an advertisement in the London Times in which she requested help in collecting used stamps so that she could paper a bedroom wall.

2 The two terms philately and philatelist, which refer to the collection and study of postage stamps, were derived from the Greek word phileo, meaning "I love" and ateleia, meaning "free of charges", in the sense that postage stamps replaced a cash postal charge. Although philately is defined in many dictionaries as the activity of collecting postage stamps, it seems that this has changed a good deal over the years, for philately has considerably developed in different directions. The era when collecting postage stamps was considered to be a simple pastime is now well past.

philatelist *n.* 集邮家   passion *n.* 爱好，酷爱
originally *adv.* 原来，最初   derive from 起源于

3 Philately is the activity of commerce and consequently has a well-established position. Moreover it has become scholarly subject. The expert concentrates on the technique, printing methods, perforations, and water-marks, while the amateur is more interested in the purpose; but for both of them, the stamp speaks the same language. While fulfilling its postal role it is the messenger which, with every item entrusted to the Post, enters households where it delivers not only the message which it carries but also culture and beauty. As a result of meticulous work of the artist and the master artisan, the postage stamp must be considered as a work of art. It possesses an immense cultural capital which, through the diversity of the subjects which it represents, covers a large part of present-day knowledge. Perhaps it was for that that philately was born — at least, it is to be hoped so.

4 Today there are millions of collectors throughout the world, millions of local, regional and national philatelic societies as well as countless periodicals and specialized catalogues. Philately has thus become at once a social phenomenon and a branch of the economy.

5 But, first of all, how do you become a philatelist? In fact who is philatelist, this person, —man, woman or child—whom we imagine sitting peacefully beneath the lamp in the evening, armed with tweezers and studying a stamp album? Why is the philatelist so carried away by these stamps which he handles with the greatest care, examines through a magnifying glass and arranges with so much affection? It would seem that basically he is just a human being like all the others but possessed of an all-devouring passion, the passion of the collector. This passion for collecting reveals itself very early, often in childhood. In fact children are very sensitive to pretty things, beautiful colors and everything completely different from their everyday surroundings. Thus the postage stamp imprinted with the mystery linked to its origin naturally arouse an interest of children, in the world of children, therefore, a small scale of collecting is created. And adults have raised it to the rank of professional activity.

6 In addition to the pleasure of satisfying his passion and finding a pleasant pastime, the collector never forgets the profitable aspect of this hobby which if well conducted, can become an extremely worthwhile financial investment.

Vocabulary Assistant

water-mark *n.* 水印
entrust *v.* 委托（运送），托付
artisan *n.* 技工，工匠
periodical *n.* 期刊
phenomenon *n.* 现象
tweezers *n.* 镊子
magnify *v.* 放大，扩大
devour *v.* 贪婪，急切地投入

amateur *n.* 业余爱好者
meticulous *adj.* 极精心的，极注意细节的
capital *n.* 资本，优势
catalogue *n.* 系列
peacefully *adv.* 平静地；和平地
be carried away 使着迷
affection *n.* 喜爱，热爱
imprint *v.* 把……印在……上

8 Complete the sentences with the following words, changing the form if necessary.

> philately   considerably   entrust   meticulous   diversity   phenomenon

1. The government has _____ the largest postal operator with the Universal Service Obligation.
2. The postal company has undergone structural transformation to offer _____ services.
3. Since the stamps came into existence, _____ has aroused public interests.
4. Integrating Marketing（全员营销）is a common _____ of the large-scaled postal companies.
5. The postal staff are _____ in dealing with the verification notes.
6. Due to the global financial crisis and electronic substitution, the mail volume has declined _____.

9 Pay attention to the italicized parts in the English sentences and translate the Chinese sentences by simulating the structure of the English sentences.

1. This would *give birth to* a passion.
   电子商务的发展使得网上快递业务应运而生。
   _____

2. Philately is the activity of commerce and consequently *has a well-established* position.
   中国邮政拥有悠久历史，因而在国内享有稳固的地位。
   _____

3. The postage stamp imprinted with the mystery linked to its origin naturally *arouse an interest* of children.
   广告邮件由于其个性化的设计和低廉的成本，引起了中小型企业的极大兴趣。
   _____

4. Adults have *raised it to the rank of* professional activity.
   监管机构把普遍服务的有关规定提升至国家法律层面。
   _____

Extended Practice

10 The following are the names of philatelic products. Please put each of them in the proper positions below its picture.

> miniature sheet   personalized stamp   special stamp   souvenir sheet
> stamp in pair   maximum card   postmark   postcard
> ordinary stamp   pre-stamped envelope   commemorative stamp
> first day cover   stamp in block   commemorative coin

 Professional Skills

13 **The following are short dialogues taking place in the post office. Use them and Postal Service Daily English provided in Unit 1 to make a COMPLETE conversation about buying philatelic products with your partner.**

购买邮品 (Buying Philatelic Products)

1. 不同面值邮票 (Stamps with Different Denominations)

   Customer: I'd like to buy some stamps.

   Clerk: In what denomination?

   Customer: 3 yuan and 1.5 yuan.

   Clerk: How many would you like of each?

   Customer: I will take 10 of each.

2. 纪念邮票 (Commemorative Stamps)

   Customer: I want to buy some commemorative stamps.

   Clerk: How about mint stamps issued recently?

   Customer: That's good! Please give me this one in blocks and those in pairs.

3. 明信片 (Postcards)

   Customer: I'd like to buy some postcards.

   Clerk: OK. We have postcards of Beijing Scenery.

   Customer: Please give me 5 sets of the Great Wall, 4 sets of the Temple of Heaven and 3 sets of the Summer Palace.

4. 其他邮品 (Other Philatelic Items)

   Customer: Would you please show me some of the philatelic products?

   Clerk: Of course. Here are the samples of souvenir sheets, souvenir folders, first day covers, pre-stamped envelopes, miniature sheets, special stamps and commemorative stamps. We also have personalized stamp albums. You can make your choices.

12 *Translate the receiver's address for correct delivery.*

Courtyard by Marriott
5950 Victoria Ave
Niagara Falls, Ontario L2G 3L7
Canada

Li Xin
30 Yuehai East Road
Gongbei, Zhuhai 519020
P. R. China

13 *Number the names of the countries according to the map, and translate them into Chinese.*

Africa

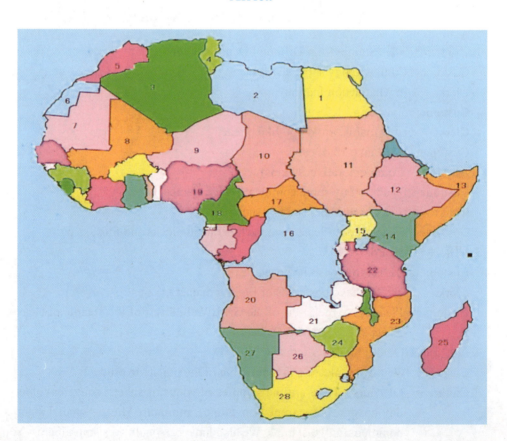

Example:
(28) South Africa ____南非____   (6) EH Western Sahara ____西撒哈拉____

( ) Chad   _____   ( ) Mali   _____
( ) Namibia   _____   ( ) Egypt   _____
( ) Algeria   _____   ( ) Tanzania   _____
( ) Botswana   _____   ( ) Cameroon   _____
( ) Angola   _____   ( ) Madagascar   _____
( ) Uganda   _____   ( ) Nigeria   _____
( ) Kenya   _____   ( ) Mauritania   _____
( ) Morocco   _____   ( ) Central Africa _____
( ) Zimbabwe   _____   ( ) Ethiopia   _____
( ) Tunis   _____   ( ) Congo   _____
( ) Libya   _____   ( ) Zambia   _____
( ) Sudan   _____   ( ) Mozambique   _____
( ) Somali   _____   ( ) Niger   _____

Get to Know the Post

Issued on May 1, 1840, in Great Britain, Penny Black is the world's first postage stamp. Before the Penny Black, the price of mailing a letter varied depending on distance and the number of sheets in the envelope. And rates weren't cheap, either. Postage could cost as much as a shilling—a day's wages for many workers. Because all mail was sent collect, thousands of letters traveled the world in vain, never to be opened.

To reform the system, British schoolmaster Sir Rowland Hill lobbied Parliament to adopt the "Penny Postage" program. For the first time, it was proposed that postage be paid in advance, using little gummed stickers to show proof of purchase. In addition, letters sent anywhere in the country would cost only a penny. The plan made sending mail affordable for nearly everybody and offered businesses tremendous savings. When presented with the Penny Postage program, many government officials feared the system would wreck the budget, claiming it would take 50 years to break even. But when the plan finally passed, the number of unpaid letters dropped so dramatically that the post office was soon profiting from the system.

Penny Black

UNIT 5 PHILATELY

 Do It Yourself

Find the English equivalents of the following Chinese from this unit.

Notebook

均一邮资 _____   黑便士 _____
邮资邮票 _____   卷票 _____
小本票 _____   邮册 _____
小型张 _____   纪念邮票 _____
面值 _____   纪念邮折 _____
首日封 _____   邮资信封 _____
个性化邮册 _____   集邮协会 _____
放大镜 _____   集邮品 _____

 OUR MISSION: Provide trusted, affordable, universal service.
— TNT

Unit 6 Direct Marketing

 Lead in

1 Watch the flash movie and discuss the following question.

1. Do you think the mail shown in the movie still junk mail? Why?
2. If you receive mail in the following shapes, what will be your reaction to them?

 Audio-Visual

2 Watch the video carefully and discuss the following questions.

1. Why can the direct mail improve the connection between customers and the company?
2. What information does the database usually have?

3 Watch the video again and fill out the blanks with what you hear.

And generally what it looks like is: you have the letter, and you have something like "dear___", and in this blank, from the database, a (1) _____ will be inserted. And when the customer receives this, it looks like they are receiving (2) _____ letter, directly to them. And the connection between the customer and you or the company is that much better, and the customers will think: wow, they send a letter (3) _____ to me. Now if you are probably cynical, you'll believe it almost (4) _____ gets this these days. But it really does (5) _____. Especially if they have been a customer of yours in the past, you can market (6) _____ to your past customers. And there is a much better rate of return than just (7) _____ these letters to anybody, and a lot of people won't have any connection to you, so they won't really (8) _____ the letter or the information in it.

Reading 1

4 Read the passage below. Fill out the blanks with the following words.

> pick   loyal   build   marketing   encourage   real   customers   service   response

Mailshots

Want to tell people about your latest product, offer or opening? Grow your reputation? Win new customers? Or simply show off your professional image? Achieve all this and more by mail.

Mailshots are a brilliant form of advertising. More and more businesses, large and small, are seeing the effectiveness of building customer relationships by post. Whether it's a "warm" personalised mailshot or a "cold" unaddressed door drop, mail can be an extremely targeted, personal and creative way to engage people.

Here we provide an insight into mail as a marketing tool.

1. Acquiring new customers

In every door there is a letterbox. Through those letterboxes are your _____, either at home or at work. The post arrives. They _____ it up. And there in their hands is your business, your image, your product or _____, your offer.

You talk to them. You tell them your news. You make them an offer. You get a _____. You close the sale. Then, over time, you keep talking to them. You _____

Vocabulary Assistant

mailshot *n.* 邮寄广告
brilliant *adj.* 杰出的；非凡的
unaddressed *adj.* （信等）不写姓名地址的，无姓名地址的
extremely *adv.* 极其地；非常地；极端地
insight *n.* 洞察力

show off 使突出；炫耀，卖弄
personalized *adj.* 个人化的；个性化的

engage *vt.* 吸引（注意力，兴趣）

relationship. They become _____, lifelong customers, buying your products and services time and time again, and recommending you to their friends.

"Yes, but that doesn't happen in the _____ world," you might be thinking. Only it does: it's called mail marketing. It can be a mailshot (personally addressed advertising) or a door drop (unaddressed advertising sent to specific postcode areas).

Mail is used by all types of businesses, in all sectors, to acquire customers, retain them and _____ them to spend more. It's a highly targeted, highly personal, highly successful form of _____.

Case Study: The Diabetic Chocolate Company
The challenge

The Diabetic Chocolate Company, a small family business producing sugar-free chocolates, wanted to drive more traffic to its website but couldn't afford to advertise.

A targeted campaign

The Diabetic Chocolate Company worked with Royal Mail to create a customer mailshot and bought an address list of 7,600 households with a diabetic resident. Because it was Christmas the mailing was designed to look like a greetings card and customers were offered £3 off their first online order. Each mailing had a promotional code to track response and pinpoint the areas where the chocolates sold well.

A great result

So far the campaign has achieved a response rate of 2.5% for the Diabetic Chocolate Company. Future mailshots can now be more targeted and the aim is to build a customer list.

2. Building customer relationships

Building profitable customer relationships means taking the opportunity to sell more products and services to customers who already know you. With Direct Mail you can target your message, be personal, relevant, engaging and memorable.

Vocabulary Assistant

sector n. 部门
retain v. 保持，保留
diabetic adj. 糖尿病患者的
target vt. 把……作为目标(或对象)
pinpoint vt. 明确指出，确定（位置或时间）；为……准确定位
profitable adj. 有利可图的，赢利的
engaging adj. 有吸引力的

acquire v. 获得，得到
traffic n. 访问量
sugar-free adj. 无糖的
campaign n. 活动

relevant adj. 相关的，适宜的
memorable adj. 容易记忆的，值得怀念的

Case Study: O2

O2 recognised a reluctance among its small and medium-sized business customers to make mobile calls abroad. The campaign was designed to challenge the preconception that

it's difficult to make calls abroad.

A 3D solution

O2 sent chopsticks to its business customers to grab their attention.

Simplicity

Certain things (like chopsticks) are difficult to use abroad. Your mobile isn't. A simple message, and a simple execution.

3. Keeping customers

Keeping customers as well as growing your own business can be a tough balancing act. It costs money and time to go out and get a new business — time and money you also want to spend on keeping your existing customers happy. Fortunately, Direct Mail offers a simple, cost-effective way to keep in touch with existing customers — and keep your bottom line protected.

Discover how other businesses have used Direct Mail to maximise their customer retention, then let us help yours to unlock the full potential of DM.

Case Study: Honda

Honda wanted to create greater customer satisfaction and improve customer retention with an engaging welcome pack.

Three-year plan

Honda devised a three-year contact strategy and sent its customers a welcome pack in the form of a storybook, introducing Honda's philosophy and explaining its Power of Dreams concept.

Happy customers

Customer satisfaction has risen from 70% to 75% since the pack was sent out.

Vocabulary Assistant

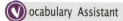

reluctance *n.* 不愿意，勉强	preconception *n.* 偏见
execution *n.* 实行，执行，实施	maximise *vt.* 最大化，增至最大限度
retention *n.* 保留，保持	pack *n.* 套装
philosophy *n.* 哲学；信条，观点	

5 **Complete the sentences with the following words, changing the form if necessary.**

| reputation | personalize | retain | promotion | recommend | acquire |

1. The postal enterprise has launched various activities to _____ its sales.
2. The sorting center _____ advanced technology to improve its efficiency.
3. In spite of fierce competition, the mail volume _____ positive growing momentum.
4. The express carrier has gained a good _____ for its high-quality services.
5. It _____ that the delivery should be finished within a definite time period.
6. The stamp show has exhibited all sorts of _____ stamps.

6 Pay attention to the italicized parts in the English sentences and translate the Chinese sentences by simulating the structure of the English sentences.

1. The Diabetic Chocolate Company wanted to *drive more traffic* to its website.
   货运代理商采用了个性化设计，增加其网站访问量。
   _____

2. Building profitable customer relationships means *taking the opportunity* to sell more products and services to customers.
   私有邮政企业抓住该契机，增加其函件业务总量。
   _____

3. *It costs money* and time to go out and get a new business.
   快递运营商花费了大量资金升级其现有车队。
   _____

4. Let us help you to *unlock the full potential of* DM.
   邮政公司充分发掘了快递业务的潜力。
   _____

Reading 2

7 Fill in the following table according to the information given in the passage below.

Product Name	
Client	
Product Function	1. to create a piece showing what makes tw telecom services different 2. _____

Product Features	Format	Design	Visual Effects	Targeted Recipients
		1. a tagline "open up to a whole new world" 2. _____ _____ 3. _____ _____ 4. a city skyline customized with local landmarks		
Results				

A Piece that Pops

tw telecom wanted its direct mail campaign to stand out. Faction Media did them one better — by creating a piece that stands up.

When you're crafting a B2B direct mail campaign, it's important that your piece has the ability to stand out on the recipient's desk. (1) What better way to accomplish that than to have the piece literally pop up?

"We wanted to create a piece showing what makes Time Warner Telecom services different; how they can add a new dimension to your ability to communicate," says Aaron Batte, principal of Faction Media, which developed the campaign for Time Warner Telecom. (The company recently changed its name to tw telecom.) "We started by adding a dimension."

Based in Littleton, Colo., tw telecom provides voice, data and Internet services to business customers in 8,500 office buildings in 75 cities nationwide. (2) Because those structures are "lit up" — that is, already connected to tw telecom's fiber-optic network — the company's spring 2008 campaign targeted other companies in the same buildings.

Specifically, Batte's creative team designed a 6×9-inch card that, on the outside, invites recipients to "open up to a whole new world" at their specific business addresses.

When they open the card, a three-dimensional city scene — complete with buildings, streets, pedestrians and a traffic signal — pops up. A prominently placed billboard offers an incentive, such as a free video camera, for making an appointment to discuss telecom service.

In the background — visible whether the card is opened or closed — is a city skyline customized with local landmarks: the Gateway Arch for St. Louise residents, the Empire State Building for New Yorkers, the Space Needle for those in the Pacific Northwest.

Vocabulary Assistant

stand out 引人注目，脱颖而出
accomplish vt. 完成，实现，达到目的
pop up 突然弹出的东西，弹出式
light up 照亮；使放光彩
pedestrian n. 步行者，行人
billboard n. 广告牌
skyline n. 地平线，以天空为背景映出轮廓
customize vt. 定制定做

craft vt. 精巧地制作
literally adv. 确实地，真正地
dimension n. 维度，范围，规模，方面
fiber-optic adj. 光纤的
prominently adv. 显著地；重要地
incentive n. 刺激；鼓励
landmark n. 地标

The campaign's response rate varies from city to city, but averages 8 percent to 10 percent, according to tw telecom. (3) <u>That's far better than the typical direct mail response rate, which historically has been closer to 1 percent to 2 percent.</u>

Why does the pop-up piece generate those kinds of returns? "It's a little larger, a little more eye-catching, a little more fun" than many direct mail pieces, says Batte. "People know there's a sales pitch in there, but this piece is saying, 'We're going to give you something back. When you engage with this piece, we're going to give you a bit of entertainment.'"

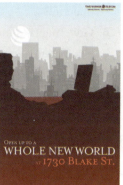

> **Vocabulary Assistant**
>
> historically *adv.* 在历史上
> eye-catching *adj.* 引人注目的；显著的
> sales pitch 兜揽生意的话，商品宣传，推销词
> generate *vt.* 产生，引起

8 *Read the above passage again, and translate the underlined sentences into Chinese.*

1. _____
2. _____
3. _____

9 *Complete the sentences with the following words, changing the form if necessary.*

> target   prominently   incentive   customize   generate   eye-catching

1. The session on the postal sector and the information society _____ some lively discussion.
2. The UPU already provides for similar quality of service _____ in respect of parcels and EMS.
3. TNT Logistics is the world leading contract logistics provider with impressive positions in _____ sectors.
4. Implementation of the project should make it possible to maintain the _____ mail collection provided to businesses.

5. Over the next few weeks, visitors to some 16,000 post offices will receive important information about how to prevent HIV through a series of _____ posters and hand-out materials.

6. Governance should play a _____ role in an age of globalization, in order to avoid a chaotic situation.

Professional Skills

10 The following are short dialogues taking place in the post office. Use them and Postal Service Daily English provided in Unit 1 to make a complete conversation about mailing printed matter with your partner.

交寄印刷品 (Mailing Printed Matter)

1. 出示内件 (Showing the contents)

   Customer: I'd like to send these books to the Netherlands as printed matter.
   Clerk: Would you please show me the contents?
   Customer: All right.
   Clerk: Thank you! By airmail?
   Customer: Airmail, please.
   Clerk: Registered?
   Customer: No.

2. 超出重量限制 (Over the Weight Limit)

   Clerk: I'm afraid that your bag is over the weight limit.
   Customer: What's the weight limit?
   Clerk: 5kg.
   Customer: What should I do then?
   Clerk: You can repack it into two bags.

11 Translate the receiver's address for correct delivery.

Swissotel Hotel Zurich
Am Marktplatz Oerlikon,
Schulstrasse 44, Zurich
Ch-8050
Switzerland

Liu Ming
No. 9 Shuaifuyuan Lane
Wangfujing St.
Beijing 100005
P. R. China

DIRECT MARKETING UNIT 6   69

12 **Number the English names of the countries according to the map, and match them with the Chinese equivalents.**

Oceania

( ) Papua New Guinea   A 所罗门群岛
( ) Australia   B 斐济
( ) Nauru   C 汤加
( ) Marshall Islands   D 澳大利亚
( ) Solomon Islands   E 新西兰
( ) Fiji   F 巴布亚新几内亚
( ) Tonga   G 瑙鲁
( ) New Zealand   H 马绍尔群岛

Get to Know the Post

It was around 1000 B.C., an Egyptian landowner wrote what is considered to be the earliest identifiable example of direct advertising. It was an advertisement on a piece of papyrus for the return of a runaway slave. The original was actually found from the ruins of Thebes and can now be seen in the British Museum. Whether or not the Egyptian landowner found his slave is unknown. Since we do not have the result to measure the effectiveness of the "return-my-slave" effort, it may be concluded that the campaign was a direct marketing failure.

History of Direct Mail

Later, the Babylonians used bricks as a means of distributing direct advertising to individuals. Guess their BPS (Babylonian Postal Service) didn't have any weight regulations for third class or bulk mail.

In 1872, Montgomery Ward launched its first catalog in the United States. Since then, direct mail has become the main tool of the marketing world. Another pioneering company in the field was R. W. Sears firm that launched its services in 1891. Both Sears and Montgomery Ward were based in Chicago, the hub of the extensive American railway system, which enabled the transfer of goods from source of production to rural communities throughout the United States.

Mail order catalogues also emerged as significant marketing tools in Europe in the late 19th century. Throughout the 20th century many companies across the world, such as IKEA and Habitat, adopted mail order as part of their daily retail sales. Mail order catalogues has become as much lifestyle guides as marketing tools.

Do It Yourself

Find the English equivalents of the following Chinese from this unit.

Notebook

商函	_____	个性化商函	_____
弹出式邮件	_____	营销工具	_____
忠实客户	_____	直复营销	_____
邮政编码	_____	数据库	_____
贺卡	_____	回复率	_____
商函促销	_____	中型企业	_____
印刷品	_____	限重	_____

 I'm right where I'm needed.

— FedEx

Unit 7 EMS and Logistics

Lead in

1 Watch the video and discuss what "The Big Idea" means and what it brought to the postal industry.

Audio-Visual

2 Watch the video and answer the following questions.

1. Why is global logistics so important?
2. What services does DHL offer?
3. Where is DHL innovation center located?

3 Watch the video again and fill out the blanks with what you hear.

Another example of what DHL has achieved is our DHL innovation center in Germany. Here research meets technology, for instance, by using (1) _____ in the development of new information tools and logistics (2) _____ devices to make things easier and more (3) _____ when controlling and delivering shipments and goods. And these are just three (4) _____ of how the DHL brand makes us one of the leaders in logistics. DHL largely (5) _____ the global network and keeps 310,000 ambitious employees busy. In fact, it is these numerous dedicated (6) _____ that keep the DHL network going.

Reading 1

4 Read the passage below. Choose the best title for each numbered paragraph.

A TNT in Chinese Domestic Market
B TNT's International Express Network in China
C TNT's Huge Growth Prospects Offered by China
D The Way Used by TNT to Strengthen its European Position
E Overview of TNT Express
F TNT's Best Way of Long-term Growth
G TNT's Market Share in Europe

TNT Express

1   TNT Express is a global player delivering shipments to over 200 countries, with fully owned operations in 64 countries. Despite the challenging economic conditions, TNT Express is continuing to see growth in several markets. This is largely due to its focus on intra-regional and domestic markets as well as on intercontinental business flows.

TNT believes that building local and regional strength is the best way to capture the long-term growth in China, India, Southeast Asia, South America, and other emerging economies. TNT thus pioneered the shift by international express companies toward interior China, India, and Brazil. Building road infrastructures inside these countries and connecting them to international routes forms the core of TNT's growth strategy.

Number one in Europe

TNT Express was created in Australia in 1946. Today, the company's home market is Europe. TNT is the B2B market leader in Europe with an 18 percent market share,

Vocabulary Assistant

intra-regional *adj.* 区域内的，地区内的	domestic *adj.* 国内的
capture *v.* 夺取，占领	emerging *adj.* 新兴的
pioneer *v.* 开辟，作先驱	shift *n.* 变化，更替
interior *adj.* 内地的，国内的	infrastructure *n.* 基础设施

followed by DHL (16%), UPS (9%) and La Poste of France (7%).

Europe still offers room for expansion. The consolidation of the market is far from finished, with countless small players making up 43% of the total. TNT is well placed to gain market shares over these competitors through its broad product portfolio, focus on customer experience, and far-reaching European road network.

2   TNT Express strives to strengthen its European position by improving the efficiency of its networks. This means replacing selected air routes with road routes, while maintaining service levels. The number and locations of hubs and depots, the pickup and delivery rounds, the composition of the air fleet, are also being reviewed to cut costs without cutting quality.

Expanding into China

The Chinese transport market offers huge growth prospects for TNT. Besides competing on the international express market, the company is building a domestic network to benefit from China's strong and resilient domestic demand.

3   TNT's international express network in China comprises 34 branches and 3 air gateways in Beijing, Shanghai, and Guangzhou. TNT offers a direct B747-400 freighter service between Shanghai and Europe four times weekly. The return flight from Liege to Shanghai includes a stopover in Singapore. In addition, TNT connects China to Vietnam, Thailand, Cambodia, Malaysia and Singapore by road, using its integrated Asia Road Network.

4   TNT has also become a leading player in the Chinese domestic market. The company introduced a nationwide, day-certain road delivery service in February 2009. It is now setting up new, modern road hubs, such as in Wuhan, central China. Domestic operations are carried out through TNT-Hoau, a trucking company that TNT bought in 2007. The acquisition has given the group ownership of the largest private road transportation network in China: 2,000 vehicles, 56 domestic hubs, and 1,260 depots, that enable to link 500 cities. These complementary networks allow TNT to offer a broad choice of services to, from, and inside China, from international air express to domestic road distribution.

Vocabulary Assistant

consolidation *n.* 整合，统一，合并
strive *v.* 争取，追求
depot *n.* 仓库，储藏所
prospect *n.* 展望，愿景
comprise *v.* 包含，构成
stopover *n.* 中途停留
acquisition *n.* 收购

portfolio *n.* 系列产品，系列服务
hub *n.* 枢纽，中心
fleet *n.* 机群，车队
resilient *adj.* 有活力的；适应力强的
gateway *n.* 口岸，关口
integrated *adj.* 综合的，整合的
complementary *adj.* 互补的，补充的

5 **Pay attention to the italicized parts in the English sentences and translate the Chinese sentences by simulating the structure of the English sentences.**

1. This *is largely due to* its focus on intra-regional and domestic markets as well as on intercontinental business flows.
   很多信件投递的延误和错误很大程度上是由于顾客既没写全地址又没有写全邮政编码。

2. The consolidation of the market *is far from* finished, with countless small players making up 43% of the total.
   邮件远不只是孤立运行的媒体，它与其他的媒体一起构成主要的通信方式。

3. *Besides* competing on the international express market, the company is building a domestic network to *benefit from* China's strong and resilient domestic demand.
   除了能够网上跟踪邮寄的包裹之外，顾客还可以受益于网上邮寄费用的折扣。

4. The Chinese transport market *offers* huge growth prospects *for* TNT.
   TNT 为客户提供快速、方便、可靠的国际投递业务。

6 **Complete the sentences with the following words, changing the form if necessary.**

> complementary   integrated   comprise   prospect   pioneer   strive

1. Easy to create, easy to mail, Ellis sent out 60 postcards to existing, dormant and _____ clients.
2. The pack _____ letter, catalogue and reply envelope.
3. Business to Business marketers see mail and e-mail playing a _____ role in the future with direct mail evolving into a more strategic role.
4. We _____ to turn every customer into a brand ambassador and we include recommend-a-friend forms both online and in our catalogue.
5. Each stamp in the set consists of a portrait of the innovator who _____ the industrial revolution.
6. Alternatively, if you don't have an eCommerce sales platform you can switch to our _____ multi-channel platform.

Reading 2

7 **Read the passage below. Fill out the blanks with the following words.**

> distribution   serve   map out   inbound   delivery   speed

UPS Supply Chain Solutions®

When you want to design your supply chain so that your business uses the most efficient methods available for sourcing, manufacturing, transportation and order fulfillment, UPS Supply Chain Solutions can be a single-source solution to meet your total logistics and distribution needs.

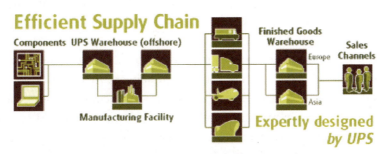

Wherever your goods must be moved or stored, we can develop the most efficient and effective way to meet your requirements. Our broad portfolio of services enables us to provide optimized and streamlined supply chain services, so you can focus on your core capabilities and on meeting your customers' expectations.

Our network of worldwide distribution facilities, combined with our global transportation services, enables same-day critical order fulfillment and returns management.

(1) Capabilities in logistics design, re-engineering and management, and service parts logistics make us the provider to turn to when you want a single, trusted source for product or parts distribution.

We offer services in:
    Order Fulfillment: Pick, Pack
    Minor Repair and Refurbishment
    Value-Added Services

Through our global network of facilities, we have the experience and the knowledge to make your business work better.

UPS gives you the ability to _____ customers of any size, anywhere, to their exact specifications. Our end-to-end _____ services include everything from _____ material flow to finished goods warehousing, inventory management, inspections, returns handling — and of course, global _____. (2) It's the full support you need to get the right products to the right places, on time and in excellent condition.

Vocabulary Assistant

efficient *adj.* 有效的，效率高的
fulfillment *n.* 完成，履行
streamline *v.* 使……简化，使……有效率
refurbishment *n.* 翻新
inventory *n.* 存货（清单）

source *v.* 寻求（尤指供货）的来源
optimize *v.* 优化
critical *adj.* 紧急的，至关紧要的
specification *n.* 规格，要求

Best of all, while we _____ your inventory through the supply chain, you'll have more time to _____ your company's next move.

Advantages

(3) <u>Whether you're part of a global company or a small but growing business, it makes sense to turn your distribution needs over to UPS.</u> Our distribution solutions can help to yield critical business benefits that crystallize throughout your company — on P&L statements, in customer satisfaction surveys, and in the ability to win the kind of business you weren't able to service in the past.

You'll conserve capital.

Why invest in infrastructure that has nothing to do with manufacturing and marketing your products? Take advantage of our established network of facilities, IT systems, and logistics experts to gain cost and service advantages. And count on our vendor-managed inventory model to improve the timing of inbound shipments, streamline stock, perfect replenishment schedules, and help to reduce carrying costs — no matter how many suppliers and end points are involved.

You'll be better positioned to serve customers.

We maintain over 35 million square feet of distribution and warehousing facilities, strategically located at approximately 1,000 sites in more than 120 countries. (4) <u>This allows for optimal staging of your inventory, which helps speed transit and lower overall transportation costs.</u> You'll get the right amount of product to the right places at the right time to meet demand.

You'll be able to plan with precision.

Our advanced IT systems provide reports and data to help optimize business planning and decisions. Have a look at inventory, orders, and shipments. Measure the product speed. Gain more visibility into the entire distribution network, and get a better sense of direction than ever before.

Vocabulary Assistant

crystallize v. 具体化，计划成型　　conserve v. 节约，节省
inbound adj. 入境的，归航的　　replenishment n. 补充（货物）
strategically adv. 战略上，颇具策略地　　optimal adj. 最佳的，最理想的
visibility n. 能见度

---

8 **Read the above passage again, and translate the underlined sentences into Chinese.**

1. _____
2. _____
3. _____
4. _____

9 Complete the sentences with the following words, changing the form if necessary.

> fulfillment   efficient   critical   specification   conserve   optimize

1. ILO and Uni Global Union representatives also contributed with their _____ expertise.
2. It adds up to DHL's existing tools to _____ routing.
3. It has also reinforced its position in special services by developing same-day business and time-_____ freight services.
4. TNT's mail division is considered one of the world's most _____ postal operators.
5. OneCode ACS _____ are available for download at mailer's convenience via a secure website.
6. The U.S. Postal Service today launched its annual _____ campaign.

Extended Practice

10 The following form includes information about TNT express in 2009. Get figures about famous international and domestic express companies. Then make a presentation.

	Mail center and hub	2,376
	Country	200
	Staff	75,500
	Mail	4,400,000

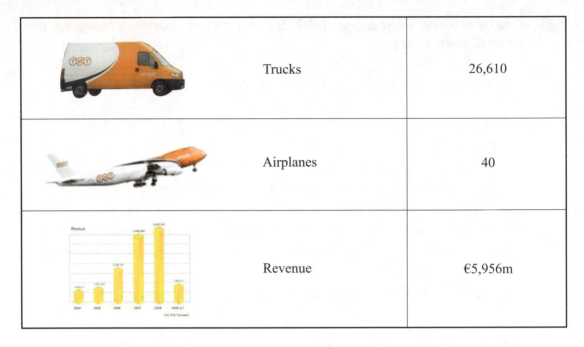

	Trucks	26,610
	Airplanes	40
	Revenue	€5,956m

11 *The following are the vehicle used by Sweden Post. Match the pictures with the names representing them.*

electric moped   electric car   mail carrier vehicle   swap body
distribution cargo van   truck and trailer   mail train   mail truck

bicycle

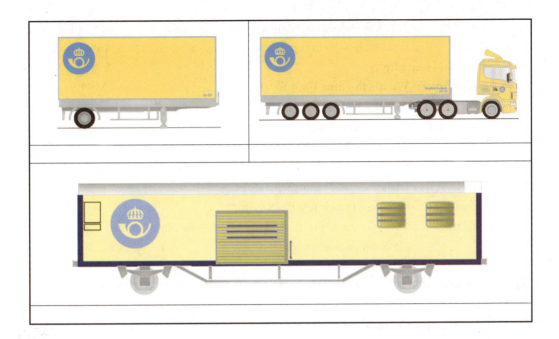

Professional Skills

 The following are short dialogues taking place in the post office. Use them and Postal Service Daily English provided in Unit 1 to make a COMPLETE conversation about mailing items by EMS with your partner.

交寄特快专递邮件 (Mailing Items by EMS)

1. 填写单式 (Filling in the Forms)
    Clerk: Please fill in this form. Press hard, please.
    Customer: Here you are.
    Clerk: Oh, please write down the name of the contents in detail here for Customs clearance, otherwise it will get delayed.

2. 收据 (Receipt)
    Customer: How much is it?
    Clerk: 295 yuan. Thank you. Here is the receipt. If you have any problems, you can make an inquiry with this receipt. Anything else?
    Customer: No, thank you.
    Clerk: You are welcome.

3. 邮件赔偿 (Compensation for EMS)
    Customer: How about the compensation if the mail is lost?
    Clerk: 400 yuan of indemnity is paid for loss or damage at no additional charge.
    Customer: If the value of the mail is more than 400 yuan, can I get more compensation?

Clerk: Yes. But before the mailing, you have to declare the value of the mail. Then you can get the compensation according to the actual value you declared.

4. 时限 (Time Limit)

Customer: What's the time limit for domestic and international EMS?

Clerk: About three days for domestic EMS and a week for international EMS.

Customer: Can you guarantee the time limit for EMS items during holidays?

Clerk: Yes. Mail can be delivered on weekends, holidays and even Spring Festival. We can ensure the delivery of your mail within the guaranteed time limit.

5. 跟踪查询 (Tracking and Tracing)

Customer: How can I track my EMS item?

Clerk: You can track your EMS item through our website, hotline 11183, SMS platform or post offices.

13 *Translate the receiver's address for correct delivery.*

Office of Conferences and Events
Bryn Mawr College
101 North Merion Avenue
Bryn Mawr, PA 19010-2899
U.S.A.

Liu Huan
NO. 4 State-owned Textile Factory
53 Kaiping Road
Qingdao, Shandong 266042
P. R. China

14 *The following are the names of city where the exchange offices are located and pictures bearing local colors of the city. Match Chinese names with the pictures and English names above.*

Japan

| Osaka | Kobe | Tokyo | Fukuoka | Yokohama |

| 东京 | 横滨 | 大阪 | 神户 | 福冈 |

India

 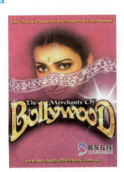 

| Delhi | New Delhi | Bombay | Calcutta |

新德里　　　　　加尔各答　　　　　德里　　　　　孟买

Australia

| Melbourne | Perth | Brisbane | Sydney |

悉尼　　　　　布里斯班　　　　　墨尔本　　　　　佩思

Switzerland

| Geneva | Zurich | Bern |

伯尔尼　　　　　日内瓦　　　　　苏黎世

Get to Know the Post

The **Pony Express** was a fast mail service crossing the North American continent from St. Joseph, Missouri, to San Francisco, California, from 1860 to 1861. It became the west's most direct means of east-west communication before the telegraph and was vital for tying gold-rich California closely with the Union just before the American Civil War.

The Pony Express was founded by William Russell, Alexander Majors, and William Waddell. To start the Pony Express, they bought 400 ponies, hired 120 riders, and built 184 stations. Relay stations were placed 10 miles apart. Every third station was a home station, where extra ponies, firearms and provisions were kept. Here, the mail would be handed over to a new rider. Majors gave each rider a Bible and required them to make oath not to swear, get drunk, gamble, treat animals cruelly or fight with other employees.

Crossing the prairies, plains, deserts and mountains, these young horsemen faced numerous dangers. They continued even at night when the only illumination came from the moon or flashes of lightening. For its 18 months of operation, it briefly reduced the time for mail to travel between the Atlantic and Pacific coasts to about ten days.

When the telegraph line was completed, there was no further need for the Pony Express. The first telegraph message from San Francisco to Washington, D.C., was transmitted on October 24, 1861. Two days later, the Pony Express came to an end.

Pony Express

 ## Do It Yourself

Find the English equivalents of the following Chinese from this unit.

Notebook

国内市场 _____   供应链解决方案 _____

发展战略	_____	退货管理	_____
市场份额	_____	增值业务	_____
削减成本	_____	库存管理	_____
国际航空快递	_____	仓储设施	_____
清关	_____	查询	_____
额外收费	_____	申报价值	_____
时限	_____	短信平台	_____

 If there's life, there is mail, and if there is mail, we are there – even on Mars or Venus.

— TNT

Unit 8 Postal Technology and Equipment

Lead in

1 Watch the video about Flats Sequencing System (FSS) and look at the flow chart. Describe the difference between the traditional mail flow and the one that uses FSS.

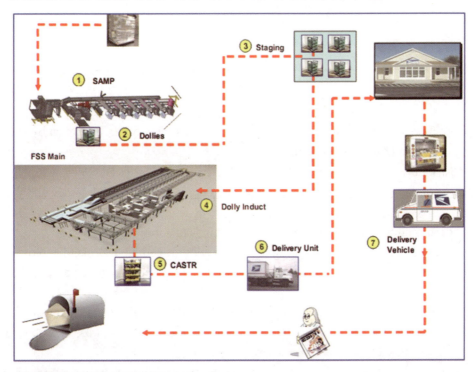

*SAMP: Stand-Alone Mail Preparation System
*CASTR: Carrier Automated Street Tray Rack

Audio-Visual

2 Watch the video and answer the following questions.

1. What does UPS Worldport refer to?
2. Why should the unloader make the package label side up?

UNIT 8 POSTAL TECHNOLOGY AND EQUIPMENT

3 **Watch the video again and fill out the blanks with what you hear.**

Before the packages (1) _____ there, they have a couple of steps to go through. Once your package is in the hands of UPS, an employee (2) _____ a smart label containing all of the shipping information. Then an employee (3) _____ the label into a system that (4) _____ it every step of the way. Next, it's off to a local UPS center to what you might (5) _____ a mini sorting. Employees quickly (6) _____ overnight packages traveling under 200 miles. They (7) _____ packages traveling farther than that into a UPS shipping pod. Then a plane (8) _____ them on the Worldport or another regional gateway.

Reading 1

4 **Read the passage below. Choose the best title for the numbered blanks.**

A People Power   B Quick Delivery   C The Technology
D Speed Wizard   E Keeping Track

Sorting the Mail

Wherever you post a letter, it's collected by a CourierPost driver and taken by truck or van to the nearest Mail Service Centre.

Most mail is sorted at night, and the Mail Service Centre is BUSY! (1) <u>Trucks and vans come and go, machines whirr and buzz, and people sort and check letters and parcels at an awesome speed.</u>

At each Mail Service Centre there are TWO kinds of sorting:

1. *Outward mail*: this is mail going to other places around New Zealand and overseas. Mostly, this mail is sorted by machine. Once sorted, it's delivered to the other Mail Service Centres for more sorting.

2. *Inward mail*: this is mail coming in from other Mail Service Centres to be delivered locally. It is sorted by people who know all the local streets and suburbs, then sent to the Local Delivery Branch or private box lobby.

(2) <u>At the Local Delivery Branch, Posties sort the mail into the precise order they'll deliver it — by streets and house numbers.</u>

 1 _____

Over the next few years New Zealand Post will be introducing exciting new machines

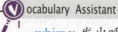 ocabulary Assistant

whirr *v.* 发出呼呼声   buzz *v.* （机器等）嗡嗡作响
awesome *adj.* 令人惊叹的   precise *adj.* 正确的，准确的

in six of its biggest Mail Service Centres. These machines will process the mail for every address in New Zealand. At the moment there are three different machines used to process the mail.

The *Culler Facer Canceller* "sees" the stamp, flips the envelopes around the same way, and cancels the stamps with an ink postmark.

At the Mail Service Centre, it reads all addresses that are clearly printed or typed. If an address is unclear it appears on a video screen for the operator to read. The operator keys in the destination code by hand, sending the item to the right sorting area without slowing the machine down.

The fastest and smartest machine of all is the *integrated mail processor* (IMP). This is a *Culler Facer Canceller*, *Optical Character Reader*, and letter sorter — all in one! The IMP sorts all the letters into different destination slots.

2 _____

The IMP can process up to 35,000 letters each hour. (3) <u>It is powered by seven computers, takes 90 seconds to finish with a letter, and carries letters at three metres a second!</u>

3 _____

Even machines can't do everything, and some outward mail is sorted by people: FastPost mail, large envelopes, packets and parcels, items without the correct stamp, and mail going overseas. Overseas mail is sorted into countries and sent to New Zealand Post's International Mail Centre in Auckland for posting overseas.

4 _____

Tracking keeps track of mail to its destination. All mail bags, trays and containers have a barcode. As they are taken to or from the Mail Service Centre, the barcode is recorded with a special hand-held scanner.

Vocabulary Assistant

flip v. 使翻转，翻转　　　　postmark n. 邮戳
destination n. 目的地　　　　slot n. 槽口

5 **Read the above passage again, and translate the underlined sentences into Chinese.**

1. _____

2. _____

3. _____

6 Complete the sentences with the following words, changing the form if necessary.

> introduce   awesome   smart   cancel   destination   precise

1. FedEx is expanding _____ post operation across U.S.
2. Since 2002 China Post had _____ home-delivery service for parcels.
3. Would it be confusing and inconvenient for postal users to pay different amounts for postage depending on the _____ of the mail?
4. Johnny was deeply impressed by the _____ designs of the stamps in the album, and has started his own stamp collection ever since.
5. A _____ forecasting of the future of mail is hard to obtain because it is difficult to account for all factors.
6. Some stamp collectors like mint stamps, while others prefer _____ stamps.

Reading 2

7 Read the numbered paragraphs of the passage below. Which paragraph does each of the following main ideas refer to?

A The reason why Flats Sequencing System will be widely used in the Postal Service.
B The commitment made by the Postal Service.
C Online services provided by the Postal Service.
D The benefits of barcode technology.

The Challenge of Emerging Technologies

1. These are challenging times for many individuals and organizations, and it is no different for the Postal Service. Regardless of any challenges, we're committed to keeping mail affordable, accessible and a powerful engine for communication and commerce.

2. For more than two centuries, we have adapted and evolved to meet the changing needs of consumers and businesses. That won't change.

3. The Postal Service has a long history of using leading-edge technologies to process and deliver mail and better serve — and connect — our customers.

Vocabulary Assistant

regardless of 无论；不管，不顾
affordable adj. 付得起的，不太昂贵的
evolve vt.&vi. 演变，进化，使发展

be committed to 以……为己任；承诺；致力于
adapt vt.&vi. （使）适应，（使）适合
leading-edge adj. （技术上）最先进的

4. We built our business on technological innovation and adaptation. As the nation has changed, so have we. From the telegraph, to the telephone, to the terabyte, the mail has complemented evolving technologies. And in the digital era, mail still plays a vital role.

5. As our customers have embraced the Internet, so have we. Our website, usps.com, is visited by more than a million people each day. It's one of the most popular sites in the federal government. Customers can do just about everything online that they can do at a Post Office. They can print shipping labels with postage, request a free package pickup, look up ZIP Codes, order packaging supplies — and much more.

6. And with our new mobile capability, some of the most popular features at usps.com are available from the growing number of mobile communications devices.

7. The Post Office? It's wherever you are. Through quick, easy and convenient online access, we also can provide customers with more information about their mail than ever before —both for large businesses that send out millions of mailpieces and for consumers who simply want to ship a package or two.

8. We marked a milestone with the launch of our Intelligent Mail services, which use barcode technology to enable business customers to track the status of their mail so they can provide better service to their customers. And the Postal Service gets important operational data to allow for mail service measurement to help us improve service for our customers. For more than 20 years, barcodes have been at the core of advances in Postal Service quality and efficiency. Automated mail processing, driven by barcodes, has allowed the Postal Service to reduce costs and deliver more rapid, reliable, and consistent service.

9. We continue to roll out the Flats Sequencing System, which is revolutionizing the way we process flat-size mail, such as magazines and catalogs, by sorting it in the order in which it's delivered by carriers. This new technology will deliver high-impact efficiency and improve mail processing, and make sure customers get even more value from the mail. Now the first of 100 flats sequencing systems has been deployed and can place mail in delivery sequence at a rate of 16,500 pieces per hour - about six pieces per second.

10. By making new technologies work for us, we help make the mail work better for our customers.

Vocabulary Assistant

terabyte n. 太字节（万亿字节，缩写为TB）
complement vt. 补足，补充
vital adj. 极重要的，必不可少的
pickup n. 提取，揽收
barcode n. 条形码
operational adj. 可用的；操作的
roll out 推出；铺开
flat-size adj. 扁平状的

era n. 时代，年代，历史时期
embrace vt. 欣然接受
milestone n. 里程碑；重大事件
status n. 情形，状况，状态
consistent adj. 一贯的，始终如一的
revolutionize vt. 使彻底变革
high-impact adj. 重大影响的

8 Complete the sentences with the following words, changing the form if necessary.

> adapt   operational   complement   embrace   consistent   deploy

1. All means of communication _____ each other.
2. The Postal Service is committed to _____ a dynamic marketplace.
3. Intelligent Mail will be fully _____ for all commercial mailers by 2010.
4. Up to now, Transportation Management program _____ 105 shipping systems into customers' mail production facilities.
5. Some mail, including First-Class Mail, Express Mail, and Priority Mail, is dependent upon _____ air transportation.
6. Postal companies _____ change in the way they respond to emerging customer needs and a rapidly evolving business environment.

9 Pay attention to the italicized parts in the English sentences and translate the Chinese sentences by simulating the structure of the English sentences.

1. *Regardless of* any challenges, we're *committed to* keeping mail affordable, accessible and a powerful engine for communication and commerce.
   不论你在多偏远的地方，我们承诺将邮件送达给你。
   _____

2. For more than two centuries, we have adapted and *evolved* to meet the changing needs of consumers and businesses.
   二十多年以来，邮政网络已发展成为一个高效的、以客户为中心的网络。
   _____

3. And in the digital era, mail still *plays a vital role*.
   今后十年，美国邮政将继续在美国人民的个人与商务生活中起着极其重要的作用。
   _____

4. We *marked a milestone with the launch of* our Intelligent Mail services.
   为了纪念我国体育史上的这 里程碑，中国邮政发行了一套以2008年北京奥运会为主题的邮票。
   _____

Extended Practice

10 The following are equipment used in mail processing centers. Find the proper name of the facilities shown below from the terms given and write them under the picture.

> letter sorting machine   flats tub   tray   parcel sorting machine
> overhead conveyor   pallet   tag   delivery sequence sorter
> hamper and cage   monotainer   mail bag

handheld scanner

Professional Skills

 The following are short dialogues taking place in the post office. Use them and Postal Service Daily English provided in Unit 1 to make a COMPLETE conversation about mailing international parcels with your partner.

交寄国际包裹 (Mailing International Parcels)

1. 禁限寄 (Not permitted to be mailed)
   Customer: I want to mail this parcel.
   Clerk: Would you please show me the contents?
   Customer: All right.
   Clerk: Thank you. Oh, it is not allowed to be sent through the post because it is dangerous item.
   Customer: All right. I will take it out.

2. 保价 (Insurance)

Clerk: Do you want to insure it?
Customer: What's the insurance fee?
Clerk: It is 1% of your insured value.
Customer: OK. I will insure it.
Clerk: Please write down the insured value here. Thank you!

12 **Translate the receiver's address for correct delivery.**

Roman-German Museum
Roncalliplatz 450667 Cologne,
North Rhine-Westphalia
Germany

To: Wang Fang
Shaanxi Materials Industry Group Corp.
9/F, No.78, Qinling North Road
Xi'an, Shaanxi 710600
P.R.China

13 **The following are the names of city where the exchange offices are located and pictures bearing local colors of the city. Put the numbers indicating the English names into the brackets of the corresponding Chinese names.**

Germany

1. Hamburg
2. Bremen
3. Koln
4. Berlin
5. Hannover
6. München
7. Leipzig
8. Bonn
9. Dusseldorf
10. Stuttgart
11. Frankfurt
12. Nurmberg

（　）柏林	（　）不来梅	（　）波恩	（　）法兰克福
（　）杜塞尔多夫	（　）汉堡	（　）汉诺威	（　）科隆
（　）慕尼黑	（　）纽伦堡	（　）斯图加特	（　）莱比锡

Get to Know the Post

In 1974, staff at Canada Post's Montreal office were noticing a considerable amount of letters addressed to Santa Claus coming into the postal system, and those letters were being treated as undeliverable. Since those employees did not want the writers, mostly young children, to be disappointed at the lack of response, they started answering the letters themselves. The amount of mail sent to Santa Claus increased every Christmas, up to the point that Canada Post decided to start an official Santa Claus letter-response program in 1983. Approximately one million letters come in to Santa Claus each Christmas, including from outside of Canada, and all of them are answered, in the same languages in which they are written. Canada Post introduced a special address for mail to Santa Claus, complete with its own postal code:

SANTA CLAUS

NORTH POLE H0H 0H0

CANADA

A Canadian postal code is a string of six characters in the format X#X #X#, where X is a letter and "#" is a single digit.

Postal Code of Santa Claus

An example is K1A 0B1, which is for Canada Post's Ottawa headquarters. The postal code H0H 0H0 is reserved for letters to Santa Claus. H0H 0H0 was chosen for this special seasonal use as it reads as "Ho ho ho". **Ho ho ho** is a rendition of a particular type of deep-throated laugh often used as the laugh of Santa Claus.

UNIT 8 POSTAL TECHNOLOGY AND EQUIPMENT

 Do It Yourself

Find the English equivalents of the following Chinese from this unit.

Notebook

保价费	_____	国际包裹	_____
扁平函件	_____	手持扫描仪	_____
出口邮件	_____	快递信件	_____
进口邮件	_____	扁平函件排序系统	_____
智能邮件	_____	综合邮件处理器	_____
邮件处理中心	_____	分信理信盖戳机	_____
国际邮件处理中心	_____	信函分拣机	_____
一体化邮件处理器	_____	光学字符识读机	_____
自动化邮件处理	_____	邮件跟踪	_____
信匣	_____	条形码	_____
邮袋	_____	货运单	_____

Every day we make the day a little brighter.

— Singapore Post

Unit 9 Postal Finance and Insurance

 Lead in

1 **Watch the video and then discuss the following questions with your classmates.**

1. What services does Western Union mainly provide according to the video?
2. How does China Post partner with Western Union?

 Audio-Visual

2 **Watch the video and answer the following questions.**

1. According to the video, what can help you when bad things happen?
2. What devastating events are mentioned in the video?
3. How can the insurance company help you recover when bad things happen?

3. Watch the video again and fill out the blanks with what you hear.

Insurance policies are very (1) _____. It's important to understand exactly what a policy covers. To have this kind of protection, you'll pay the insurance company over time. Even if you're healthy and your property is safe, you'll still pay on a regular basis. These payments are how insurance companies can (2) _____ to cover people like you. Here's what I mean. You are one of thousands who are paying the insurance company on a (3) _____ basis. The company takes this money and pools it together. When bad things happen to policy holders, the company has enough money to help them recover as (4) _____ in the policy.

Of course, this means you may pay for insurance your whole life and never use it. Before you question the value, remember that insurance covers the big (5) _____ caused by things that are out of your (6) _____. Without insurance, these things can come along and take away your hard-earned money. Insurance is an important part of being (7) _____ with your money and (8) _____. Talk with a company you trust about what's important to you. Take the time to ask questions, read the fine print and compare policies. Insurance won't keep you from falling in, but it will help you recover more easily when bad things happen.

Reading 1

4. Read the passage below. Choose the best title for each numbered paragraph.

A Operation Support Centers.
B ATMs and Internet Banking
C Branch Network
D Computer Centers
E Customer Centers

Japan Post Bank

Japan Post Bank began operating on October 1, 2007, but its operations trace back to 1875 when postal money order and postal savings services were launched by Hisoka Maejima, now known as the founding father of Japan's modern postal services.

(1) Prior to establishing a postal system in Japan, Maejima spent time in the United Kingdom studying its long-standing postal system, which was implemented in 1840.

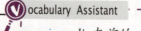ocabulary Assistant

prior *adj.* 在前的；居先的   implement *v.* 实施；执行

During his studies, he found that the post offices in the United Kingdom were not involved solely in the postal business but also were carrying out postal money order and savings services. When he returned to Japan to establish the country's first postal system, he also introduced postal money order and savings services.

Now Japan Post Bank continues the successful operations of Japanese postal savings services as part of the privatization for Japan Post's four businesses — postal savings services, insurance services, postal services, and over-the-counter services — under the Postal Service Privatization Law.

1 _____

(2) Japan Post Bank has a total of 24,086 outlets, comprising a retail network of 233 directly operated branches and nearly 24,000 post offices extending throughout Japan. These outlets provide individual customers with savings account, settlement, and other basic banking products and services and boast a deposit base of approximately ￥180 trillion at March 31, 2009.

Administration Service Centers

The administration service centers provide data processing services for all outlets in order to reduce the burden of back office operation. The centers check and organize many documents used by the branches and post offices, issue and renew bank passbooks and ATM cards, input direct deposits of employee wages and automatic transfer data, and compile settlement and statistical data.

2 _____

Japan Post Bank has 49 operation support centers set up throughout Japan. Their primary responsibility is to provide support in maintaining and improving the quality of each agency's operations. (3) In addition to responding to inquiries about administrative processing methods from agencies the centers keep track of agencies' administrative processing and provide guidance.

Vocabulary Assistant

solely *adv.* 单独地，仅仅
extend *v.* 延伸，扩大
trillion *n.* 万亿
processing *n.* 处理
compile *v.* 收集，汇编
administrative *adj.* 行政的，管理的

privatization *n.* 私有化，民营化
settlement *n.* 清算，结账
administration *n.* 管理，行政
passbook *n.* 银行存折
statistical *adj.* 统计的
guidance *n.* 引导，指导

3 _____

The Bank has two computer centers that provide online services in real time such as storage of transaction data and interest calculations. As part of the business contingency plan, they have a backup center in a different location to prevent interruption of service during a major earthquake or similar events.

4 _____

Japan Post Bank has the nation's largest ATM network with 26,136 machines spread throughout the country. Their goal is to make ATMs easy for anybody to use.

- **Aiming at the Most User-Friendly ATMs**

(4) The ATMs are designed to be at a comfortable height with ramps for the customers in wheelchairs and have Braille operating instructions, keyboards, and ATM cards for the visually impaired customers. Also, through interphones attached to the ATMs or earphones, customers are able to receive instructions and information on operations, remittance amounts, or account balances.

- **Providing Convenience for Foreign Visitors**

The machines accept foreign credit and ATM cards for visitors to take out local currency conveniently. Moreover, operating instructions are available in English, making it easy for foreign visitors to use the machines.

- **Accepted cards**

VISA, VISAELECTRON, PLUS, MasterCard, Maestro, Cirrus, American Express, Diners Club, JCB, China Unionpay

Internet Banking

Now Japan Post Bank considers launching Internet banking to supplement or replace their branches, agency offices and ATMs in the future.

By taking advantage of the nationwide network of post offices, Japan Post Bank aims to offer comprehensive financial services to a wide range of individuals, thereby achieving a retail business model that makes it the most convenient and dependable bank in Japan.

Vocabulary Assistant

contingency n. 意外事故，偶然事件
interruption n. 中断，阻碍
Braille n. 盲文字符
impair v. 削弱，减少
remittance n. 汇款，汇寄
VISA 维萨卡，维信卡
Maestro 万事顺卡
American Express 美国运通卡
JCB 吉士美卡(日财卡)
supplement v. 补充，增补

backup n. 灾备；后援
ramp n. 斜坡，坡道
visually adv. 视觉上
interphone n. 内部电话，对讲机
balance n. 结余，余额
MasterCard 万事达卡
Cirrus 顺利卡
Diners Club 大来卡
China Unionpay 中国银联
comprehensive adj. 综合的，广泛的

5 **Read the above passage again, and translate the underlined sentences into Chinese.**

1. _____
2. _____
3. _____
4. _____

6 **Complete the sentences with the following words, changing the form if necessary.**

| implement | prior | remittance | impair | contingency | balance |

1. You are requested to furnish us with the name of your bank _____ to the conclusion of the first transaction between us.
2. Australia Post new website meets accessibility standards for visually _____ users.
3. What measures can be _____ to improve postal security?
4. They have to raise additional capital and cut dividends to help improve their _____ sheet.
5. Last year around £90 billion was _____ through the outlets of Post Office®.
6. A fire in our warehouse was a _____ that we had not expected.

Reading 2

7 **Read the passage below. Fill out the blanks with the following words.**

| calculate | applies | close | insured | base | cover | against |

How Does Insurance Work?

Insurance exists because risk exists. There is a possibility that anyone could become a victim of fire, theft, auto accidents, other injury accidents, illness, severe weather, lawsuits and more. We are subject to risk at home, at work, in our cars, traveling, in the hospital or anywhere at any time.

Vocabulary Assistant

victim n. 受害人   lawsuit n. 诉讼
subject adj. 易受……的；倾向于……的

Transfer of Risk

Insurance cannot remove the risk or the likelihood that one might become a victim of any of these events, but what it does is transfer all or some of the financial impact of any of these events. Insurance exists to help individuals recover from the financial consequences of these events by pooling the resources of a large group to pay for the losses of a small group.

A Little Background about Insurance

Insurance has been around in some form since traders first began to travel over water  to trade their goods. There is documented evidence that Chinese and Babylonian traders began to protect themselves against risk as far back as the 3rd century BC. Traders realized that if they spread their goods among multiple vessels, rather than putting all of their cargo on one vessel, they had a better chance of avoiding complete loss.

In later years, shippers in Great Britain reasoned that if 100 ship owners each chipped in money, if some of those ships were damaged or lost, the money collected from all 100 ships could be used to repair or replace the few. Extreme losses following the Great Fire of London in 1666 led to the creation of the world's first actual insurance company, The Insurance Office, or The Fire Office.

Law of Large Numbers

In order to afford to _____ the financial losses of its customers, an insurance company needs a very large _____ of members. For each different type of loss that they insure _____, insurance companies have years of statistics that help them _____ how many losses they are likely to have. They are counting on the law of large numbers which, when applied to insurance, states that the more members in an _____ group, the more likely it is that the number of actual losses will be very _____ to the number of expected losses. This law also _____ to gambling casinos.

Vocabulary Assistant

likelihood *n.* 可能性　　　　　　　　consequence *n.* 结果，后果
pool *v.* 汇集，集中；共享　　　　　be around 出现，露面
document *v.* 用文件证明；为……提供文件(或证据等)
Babylonian *adj.* 巴比伦的　　　　　as far back as 早在……
multiple *adj.* 多样的，多个的　　　vessel *n.* 船；容器
cargo *n.* 货物　　　　　　　　　　　reason *v.* 推论；劝说
replace *v.* 代替，替换　　　　　　　statistics *n.* 统计，统计数字
count on 指望，依靠　　　　　　　　gambling casino 赌场

Determining Payments

The insurance that each member of the insured "pool" has to pay is different and is based on many factors. For life and health insurance, for example, the insured person's age is the most important factor. It is statistically provable that younger people have fewer claims for life and health (except for pregnancy and childbirth), so their insurances will be lower than an older person or someone with health issues.

For car insurance, the driver's age, gender, geographic location, type of car and driving history all factor in to the amount they will have to pay for insurance coverage. Teenagers have to pay higher auto insurance rates because statistical history has proven that they have more accidents with higher losses than a 40 year old driver. The larger the pool of insured is, the more the risk is spread out, and the lower the rates can be.

These same principles of transferring risk and the law of large numbers also apply to business insurance, liability insurance, accident insurance, specialty insurance and more.

So in order to remain viable, an insurance company needs at least 3 basic things:

- A large pool of insured in a diverse demographic (age, gender, health, location, occupation, history);
- Reliable, current statistics on the probability of loss for each type of insurance offered;
- Sufficient payments to cover the anticipated losses.

Vocabulary Assistant

provable *adj.* 可证明的
pregnancy *n.* 怀孕
factor in 将……纳入、列入为重要因素（尤指作预测或计划时）
coverage *n.* 保险项目，覆盖范围
diverse *adj.* 多种多样的，不同的
occupation *n.* 职业
claim for 要求（赔偿）
gender *n.* 性别
liability *n.* 责任，义务
demographic *adj.* 人口统计学的
anticipated *adj.* 预料的，预期的

8 **Pay attention to the italicized parts in the English sentences and translate the Chinese sentences by simulating the structure of the English sentences.**

1. We *are subject to* risk at home, at work, in our cars, traveling, in the hospital or anywhere at any time.
   包装不当，邮件容易在运输途中受到损坏。

2. There is documented evidence that Chinese and Babylonian traders began to *protect* themselves *against* risk as far back as the 3rd century BC.
   牢靠的密码有助于保护你的网上账户免受入侵者(intruder)的入侵。

3. They are *counting on* the law of large numbers.
   个人和中小企业可以依靠邮政储蓄银行获得小额信贷(microfinance)。

4. *If* they spread their goods among multiple vessels, *rather than* putting all of their cargo on one vessel, they *had a better chance of* avoiding complete loss.

如果你选择邮政特快专递而不是求助于小型速递公司，你就更能够获得安全、可靠的服务。

_____

9 *Complete the sentences with the following words, changing the form if necessary.*

| premium | diverse | replace | cover | document | occupation |

1. The Health Care Reform Bill is intended to expand insurance _____ largely for middle-class and poor families.
2. He paid _____ on his life insurance last year.
3. The delivery of freight during the day is _____ by signature of the recipient as usual.
4. We not only treat each other with respect but encourage _____ in our workforce.
5. We continue to look for energy-efficient _____ vehicles for our aging fleet.
6. Both facilities _____ an area four times the size of the previous premises.

Extended Practice

10 *The following are the abbreviations and logos of different banks. Match the abbreviations with the logos and put the abbreviations into Chinese.*

| CCB | HSBC | ICBC | CMB | BCM | CEB |
| ABC | CMBC | BOB | CIB | GDB | |

BOC（中国银行）		

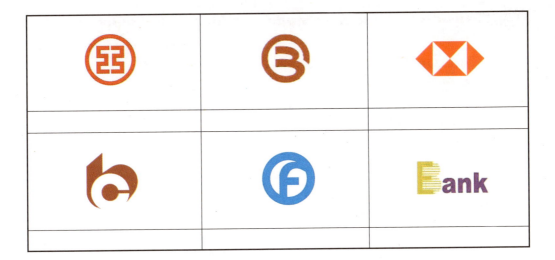

Professional Skills

 The following are short dialogues taking place in the post office. Use them and Postal Service Daily English provided in Unit 1 to make a COMPLETE conversation about international remittance with your partner.

国际汇兑 (International Remittance)

1. 汇款 (Sending Money)

   Customer: I would like to send 1,000 dollars to Hong Kong.

   Clerk: Would you please show me your ID card? Thank you. Please fill out these forms.

   Customer: Here you are. How much is the transfer fee?

   Clerk: 20 dollars. Please check the relevant information and sign your name.

   Customer: No problem.

   Clerk: Keep your receipt and remember your Money Transfer Control Number, please.

2. 收汇 (Receiving Money)

   Customer: I want to get my money.

   Clerk: Would you please show me your ID card? Thank you. Fill out these forms, please.

   Customer: Here you are.

   Clerk: Thank you. Do you want to take US dollars or RMB?

   Customer: What's the exchange rate?

   Clerk: I'll check it. Nearly 6.82.

   Customer: I would like to take RMB.

3. 兑付最高限额 (The Maximum Amount for Cashing)

   Customer: What's the highest limit for cashing by Western Union each day?

   Clerk: 10,000 dollars.

12 **Translate the receiver's address for correct delivery.**

Head Office
Japan Post Holdings Co., Ltd.
1-3-2 Kasumigaseki, Chiyoda-ku
Tokyo, 100-8798
Japan

To: Miss Li Li
   Jiangsu Shinri Machinery Co., Ltd.
   No. 20 Fengqi Road
   Wujin Hi-Tech Industrial Zone
   Changzhou, Jiangsu 213166
   P. R. China

13 **The following are the names of city where the exchange offices are located and pictures bearing local colors of the city. Match Chinese names with the pictures and English names above.**

Russia

Vladivostok	Moscow	St. Petersburg
莫斯科	圣彼德堡	海参崴

France

Paris	Strasbourg	Marseille
斯特拉斯堡	马赛	巴黎

Italy

Milan	Torino	Rome	Venice	Genoa
罗马	威尼斯	热那亚	米兰	都灵

Britain

Dover	Birmingham	Liverpool	London	Coventry	Manchester
伦敦	考文垂	伯明翰	多佛尔	曼彻斯特	利物浦

Get to Know the Post

The courier picture on the postal savings card, originated from the brick painting of Wei-Jin period, has existed for over 1600 years.

Dressed up in black hat, short robe and a pair of high boots, the courier on the horseback is holding the horse's reins in one hand and documents in the other, riding at full gallop. The horse's tail is swinging high because of the fast speed, whereas the courier remains extraordinarily calm on the horseback.

This illustration vividly conveys the sense of urgency involved in postal relay in border area at that time, and records the exact setting of the earliest postal service in China.

A close inspection of the courier's face on the painting reveals that he has no mouth! This perplexing feature implies the importance of confidentiality in postal relay. Still, this concept pervades today's postal services, many more ideas such as security and reliability of postal savings have also emerged from it.

Ancient Courier

In 1995, this courier image was selected to "endorse" the postal savings card, which highlights both the long history of China post and the special feature of communication.

 Do It Yourself

Find the English equivalents of the following Chinese from this unit.

Notebook

保险费　_____　　索赔　_____
承保范围　_____　　保险费率　_____
商业保险　_____　　责任保险　_____
意外伤害保险　_____　　专业保险　_____
预计损失　_____　　邮政汇票　_____
邮政储蓄业务　_____　　储蓄账户　_____
结算　_____　　存款基础　_____
后台运作　_____　　交易数据　_____
利息计算　_____　　汇率　_____
灾备中心　_____　　账户余额　_____
网上银行　_____　　国际汇兑　_____
汇款单　_____　　手续费　_____
汇款监控号　_____　　取款单　_____

We make a lifetime commitment to our customers, forming a mutual bond of trust.

— Japan Post Bank

Unit 10 Social Responsibility

 Lead in

1 **Watch the video and answer the following questions.**

1. How did the early mail carriers deliver mail? What about now?
2. What do the vehicles in the short video have in common? Why do you think they are becoming more and more popular?
3. What else can we do to protect the environment in our daily life?

 Audio-Visual

2 **Watch the introductory part to Deutsche Post's taking responsibilities and answer the following questions.**

1. What is the motto of Deutsche Post?
2. What are the three programs Deutsche Post focuses on?

3 **Watch the part of GoGreen and fill in the blanks.**

One of the major causes of climate change is rising green house gas emissions, so Deutsche Post aims to face (1 what) _____ and improve CO_2 efficiency by (2 how much) _____. Measures taken include using (3 what kind) _____ technologies, reducing energy consumption, testing innovative technology for (4 what) _____, optimizing (5 what) _____, and involving (6 whom) _____ as well as their subcontractors.

4 Watch the part of GoHelp and fill in the blanks.

Natural disasters often affect (1 whom) _____. Deutsche Post DHL set up Disaster Response Teams to provide with help (2 how) _____. When natural disaster happens, one of the (3 how many) _____ regional teams can react within (4 how long) _____ and employee volunteers support with incoming (5 what) _____ at airport closest to the affected region.

5 Watch the part of GoHelp again and answer the following questions.

1. When did Deutsche Post DHL have the idea of setting up Disaster Response Teams?
2. What kind of program did Deutsche Post set up to solve the chaos at the airport?

6 Watch the part of GoTeach and answer the following questions.

1. Why does DHL carry out GoTeach program?
2. What kind of people does Deutsch Post especially support?

Reading 1

7 Match the headings of Column A with the contents of Column B.

Column A	Column B
1. Greening the Mail	A. signs to remind customers to place used mail into recycling bins
2. Carrier Pickup	B. use compressed natural gas or other fuels, streamline delivery routes to reduce driving time and fuel use
3. Mail Back Program	C. use recyclable packages and envelopes
4. Read, Respond and Recycle	D. provide free recycling envelopes for customers to discard used or obsolete small electronic products
5. Greener Stamps	E. use water-based inks and nontoxic biodegradable adhesives
6. Alternative Fuel Vehicles	F. combine delivery and pickup

Leaving a Green Footprint

The global postal network is the world's largest physical distribution network. Every day, postal services deliver billions of pieces of mail processed in thousands of post offices using as many vehicles, motorcycles, airplanes, boats and trains. What's more, the post offices and 5.5 million postal employees consume electricity, water and paper, which all have an impact on the environment.

In recent years, postal services have come to realise the effect their business has on the environment. In their efforts to protect the environment, postal services world-wide are embarking on recycling programmes, introducing environment-friendly products, using recycled material and participating in various environment awareness programmes. Postal administrations also issue postage stamps that promote the environment, endangered species and nature and wildlife conservation. A number of postal services have also started experimenting with alternative transport energy systems to reduce pollution.

The USPS is committed to environment stewardship. They know that what's good for the planet is also good for its business. Its business can only benefit by doing what's right for future generations. Let's look at what the United States Postal Service (USPS) is doing to protect the environment.

Greening the mail

More than a half-billion packages and envelopes provided to customers by the USPS annually are nearly 100 percent recyclable and created using environmentally friendly materials. They are the only shipping company that has earned Cradle-to-Cradle certification for the environmentally friendly design and manufacturing of its shipping boxes and envelopes.

All suppliers providing USPS boxes, envelopes and other certified materials must also adhere to Cradle-to-Cradle standards.

Vocabulary Assistant

consume v. 使用，消耗
in one's effort 在……努力下
species n. 物种
alternative adj. 可供替代的
be good for 对……有益
Cradle-to-Cradle certification 从摇篮到摇篮认证
manufacture v.（大规模）制造，生产
adhere v. 遵循，依照

impact n. 影响，作用
embark v. 着手，开始从事
conservation n. 保护
stewardship n. 管理工作

certified adj. 合格的

Carrier Pickup

USPS has helped the customers reduce their carbon footprint by providing expanded Carrier Pickup service — going to customers' doors during their normal delivery day to pick up their outgoing packages.

Mail Back Program

As part of its "Saving of America's Resources (SOAR)" initiative, the USPS is partnering with various companies to help recycle and dispose of certain types of products.

The Mail Back program makes it easier for customers to discard used or obsolete small electronics in an environmentally responsible way. Customers use free envelopes available in 1,500 Post Offices to mail back inkjet cartridges, Black Berries, digital cameras, iPods, cell phones and MP3 players without paying any postage. Keeping electronics out of landfills is a smart move since some contain toxic materials, including lead, cadmium, and mercury that can leak into the soil and ground water.

In 2009, customers used the Mail Back envelopes to recycle nearly 152,000 pounds of material.

Read, Respond and Recycle

USPS is encouraging customers to "read, respond and recycle". In 8,000 Post Offices nationwide, signs remind PO Box customers to open their mail, take whatever action is necessary and place the waste in recycling bins.

Greener Stamps

The USPS uses water-based inks to print stamps and nontoxic, biodegradable adhesives.

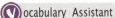

Vocabulary Assistant

carbon *n.* 〈化〉碳
initiative *n.* 倡议，新方案
dispose *v.* 处置，处理
obsolete *adj.* 废弃的，过时的
cartridge *n.* 墨粉鼓
toxic *adj.* 有毒的
cadmium *n.* 〈化〉镉
leak *v.* 泄漏
water-based *adj.* 以水为基的
biodegradable *adj.* 可以进行生物降解处理的
adhesive *n.* 胶水，粘合剂

expanded *adj.* 扩展的
partner *v.* 做伙伴，同……合作
discard *v.* 丢弃
inkjet *n.* 喷墨
landfill *n.* 垃圾填埋场
lead *n.* 〈化〉铅
mercury *n.* 〈化〉汞
bin *n.* 箱，仓
nontoxic *adj.* 无毒的

Alternative Fuel Vehicles

USPS also uses refined bio-based oil, alternative fuels such as compressed natural gas, hydrogen, or ethanol gas, and re-tread tires on their fleet of Postal vehicles. They're constantly streamlining their delivery routes to reduce driving time and fuel use.

On the eve of the 40th anniversary of Earth Day, the U.S. Postal Service unveiled its green newsroom, a one-stop shop for all its environmental information.

"At the Postal Service's green newsroom, every day is Earth Day," said Sam Pulcrano, vice president, Sustainability. "We hope America visits the new green newsroom, and usps.com/green, to learn more about the Postal Service's commitment to the environment."

Vocabulary Assistant

refined *adj.* 精炼的，精良的	bio-based *adj.* 生物产品的
compressed *adj.* 压缩的	hydrogen *n.* 〈化〉氢
ethanol *n.* 〈化〉乙醇	re-tread *adj.* 翻新的
tire *n.* (tyre)轮胎	on the eve (of) 在……前夕
unveil *v.* 使公之于众，公布	sustainability *n.* 可持续性

8 *Pay attention to the italicized parts in the English sentences and translate the Chinese sentences by simulating the structure of the English sentences.*

1. *In their efforts to* protect the environment, postal services world-wide are embarking on recycling programmes.
   为了千方百计降低成本，该协会采用了黑白印刷的标准信封（standard size envelope）。
   _____

2. They know that *what's good for* the planet *is also good for* its business.
   他们知道对社区有益的事情对自己也有益。

3. The USPS *is partnering with* various companies to help recycle and dispose of certain types of products.
   美国邮政正在与各大公司和社会团体合作开展"回寄"活动，回收电子垃圾（e-waste）。

4. The Mail Back program *makes it easier for* customers to discard used or obsolete small electronics in an environmentally responsible way.
   美国邮政开办的邮箱在线业务（PO Boxes Online）更方便顾客通过互联网申办和管理自己的邮箱。

5. USPS encourages customers to *take whatever action is necessary* to recycle waste materials.
   美国邮政的任务是采取任何必要措施继续提供普遍服务。

9 Complete the sentences with the following words, changing the form if necessary.

unveil   adhere   leak   consume   dispose   sustainability

1. The Postal Service achieved significant savings in energy _____ from the use of alternative fuel vehicles.
2. It is essential for UPU member countries _____ to international standards in order to cooperate in the postal field.
3. Japan Post _____ a list of cost cutting measures, including closing some postal hotels.
4. Removing recyclables (可回收物) from trash reduces landfill volume as well as trash _____ costs.
5. The Royal Mail has launched its new environmental strategy for achieving _____ growth.
6. They are liquid substance, so you'd better put some cotton or sponge around them in case of _____.

Reading 2

10 Read the passage below. List the actions TNT took to reduce CO_2 emissions.

Example: 1. Optimising the road networks
2. _____
3. _____
4. _____
5. _____

Taking Responsibility

Taking responsibility is an integral part of TNT's practices. The company's efforts have gained external recognition. A member of the Dow Jones Sustainability Index, TNT not only leads the "industrial transportation" sector and the "Industrial Goods and Services" super sector, but also boasts the highest score of all companies included in the index.

All TNT's Express operations are certified to five standards: Investors in People (training and employee development), ISO 9001 (quality), ISO 14001 (environment),

Vocabulary Assistant

integral adj. 构成整体所必需的，不可或缺的   external adj. 外界的
boast v. 有(引以为荣的事物)，自夸   investor n. 投资者

OHSAS 18001 (health and safety) and SA 8000 (labour standards and personnel rights in non-OECD countries).

TNT's corporate social responsibility policy is best expressed by two programmes: TNT's partnership with the United Nations World Food Programme (WFP) and "Planet Me," the group's answer to global warming.

Green Ways to Move the Mail

Working to reduce CO_2 emissions

Pledging to cut one's CO_2 emissions is often heard these days. (1) However, when you are one of the world's largest road and air transport companies, this is no small promise. The transport industry alone produces one fifth of the world's carbon emissions.

To this end, TNT in 2007 launched a company-wide initiative called "Planet Me." It comprises CO_2 reduction measures in the company's eight most important operational areas: aviation, buildings, business travel, company cars, partnering with customers, operational fleet, procurement, and investments. "Planet Me" also stimulates employees to use less energy at home and on the road.

The Express division fully takes part in this effort. Examples of actions include:

• Optimising the company's road networks to drive less kilometres and avoid driving empty trucks or vans.

• Training drivers and managers alike to safe and economic driving.

• Using electric vehicles. For instance, TNT Express UK runs 50 zero-emission electric vehicles for its UK inner-city operations. The battery-driven 7.5-ton Newton trucks from Smith Electric Vehicles are exempt from the London congestion charge. (2) They incur no road tax and it costs just GBP 25 a week to recharge the battery, as opposed to GBP 110 spent on fuel for a diesel vehicle. TNT expects these trucks to outperform the operational life of their diesel equivalent, returning a seven-year operating life.

• Testing vehicles running on bio-fuels, hybrids, biogas and hydrogen related technologies.

• Working with the aircraft industry and airports to reduce emissions from air

Vocabulary Assistant

emission *n.* 排放物
aviation *n.* 航空，航空制造业
procurement *n.* （尤指为政府或机构）采购，购买
investment *n.* 投资
optimise *v.* 使最优化
congestion *n.* 拥挤
as opposed to (sth) 与……形成对照
diesel *n.* 柴油
hybrid *n.* 混合物，生成物

pledge *v.* 保证，发誓
stimulate *v.* 激发，促进
be exempt from 免于
incur *v.* 招致
GBP 英镑
bio-fuel *n.* 生物燃料
biogas *n.* 生物气（尤指沼气）

transport. TNT Express is working with the Liege airport to optimise the planes' departures.

Fighting hunger and supporting emergency relief logistics

(3) TNT has supported the United Nations World Food Programme (WFP), the world's largest humanitarian aid agency, since 2002. Each year, WFP provides food to some 90 million people in 80 countries. Over the past five years, TNT has contributed €29.4 million to WFP operations, not including TNT employees' contribution of €9 million.

TNT's contribution includes knowledge transfer, awareness campaigns, and fundraising projects. Moreover, the company provides hands-on support (transport, warehousing, and personnel) to WFP in countries hit by disaster. In 2008, TNT helped respond to emergencies in Myanmar, Haiti, and India (Bihar). The same year, the Group also performed transport optimisation projects in Mali and Ethiopia.

(4) In addition, TNT has agreed with UPS and Agility Logistics to deploy joint "Logistics Emergency Teams" in countries hit by major natural disasters, if requested by the United Nations Global Logistics Cluster, a group of humanitarian agencies led by WFP.

Vocabulary Assistant

Liege 列日（比利时城市名）
relief *n.* 救济，救援物品
transfer *n.* 传递，转移
Myanmar 缅甸
Bihar 比哈尔(印度邦名)
humanitarian *adj.* 人道主义的
hands-on *adj.* 动手的，实际操作的
Haiti 海地
optimisation *n.* (optimization) 最优化

11 **Complete the sentences with the following words, changing the form if necessary.**

> pledge   emission   investment   comprise   optimise   relief

1. The USPS work force is _____ of employees from different cultures, with Black people taking up 21% of its staff.
2. Deutsche Post is busy with shipping food, water, satellite telephones, flashlights and batteries to _____ the great pain among the quake victims.
3. We will continue to _____ funds to maintain our infrastructure, including facilities, vehicles, and technology systems.
4. We are testing hybrid and fuel cell-powered vehicles, which _____ pure water from their tailpipes.
5. _____ the processing network like this will help the Postal Service keep the cost of postage affordable for the customers.
6. China Post makes a _____ to cut CO_2 emission in order to protect the environment.

12 *Read the above passage again, and translate the underlined sentences into Chinese.*

1. _____
   _____
2. _____
   _____
3. _____
   _____
4. _____
   _____

Professional Skills

13 *The following are short dialogues taking place in the post office. Use them and Postal Service Daily English provided in Unit 1 to make a COMPLETE conversation about Mail Packing with your partner.*

邮件的封装 (Mail Packing)

1. 更换包装箱 (Changing the Packing Box)
   Clerk: I'm afraid that you have to change your packing box, because it is not strong enough.
   Customer: Do you have packing boxes here for sale?
   Clerk: Yes.
2. 画的包装 (Packing of Painting)
   Customer: How to pack this Chinese painting?
   Clerk: We have mail tubes here.
3. 易碎物品的包装 (Packing of Fragile Articles)
   Customer: I want to post this tri-coloured glazed pottery of the Tang Dynasty to Italy.
   Clerk: It's fragile article. Please put cushioning material between and around them to prevent any friction or knocks during transport.
   Customer: Can I buy them here?
   Clerk: Yes.

14 *Translate the receiver's address for correct delivery.*

BANK OF FINLAND
P.O. Box 160
FI-00101 HELSINKI
FINLAND

To: Jia Jun
　　Beijing Teamsun Technology Co., Ltd.
　　Floor 10th, Building A, Science Fortune Center
　　No. 8 Xueqing Rd, Haidian District
　　Beijing 100085
　　P. R. China.

15 *The following are the names of city where the exchange offices are located and pictures bearing local flavor of the city. Put the numbers indicating the English names into the brackets of the corresponding Chinese names.*

United States of America

1. Oakland　2. Washington　3. Detroit　4. Philadelphia　5. Miami

6. San Francisco　7. Honolulu　8. Portland　9. Atlanta　10. Denver

11. Dallas　12. New Orleans　13. Chicago　14. Seattle　15. New York

16. Houston　17. Kansas City　18. Los Angeles　19. Boston

SOCIAL RESPONSIBILITY UNIT 10 117

（ ）华盛顿	（ ）纽约	（ ）旧金山	（ ）波士顿	（ ）底特律
（ ）芝加哥	（ ）丹佛	（ ）迈阿密	（ ）休斯敦	（ ）达拉斯
（ ）洛杉矶	（ ）费城	（ ）奥克兰	（ ）西雅图	（ ）波特兰
（ ）亚特兰大	（ ）新奥尔良	（ ）堪萨斯城	（ ）火奴鲁鲁	

Get to Know the Post

• Regularly update and improve your mailing lists to limit duplication and waste.

• Use research to effectively target your customers. Folks who live in apartment buildings, for example, probably don't need lawn services.

• Allow customers to opt out of your mailings to ensure you're not sending them unwanted mail.

• Use recycled materials for the mailings you create.

• When sourcing paper, make sure that it comes from forests managed with practices certified by independent, third-party organizations.

• Design your mailings to be recyclable, too, by printing with water-based inks, on uncoated paper stocks, and sending windowless envelopes. Print on both sides of the paper to save resources and reduce mailing costs.

• Encourage your customers to recycle the mailing once they've read it, and tell them how you made your mailing as green as possible.

Green Ideas for Mailers

Do It Yourself

Find the English equivalents of the following Chinese from this unit.

Notebook

邮政网络 _____   有毒材料 _____   _____
再生材料 _____   濒危物种 _____
替代燃料 _____   邮政车辆 _____

投递路线	_____	企业社会责任	_____
电动车辆	_____	喷墨打印机墨盒	_____
实物配送网络	_____	碳足迹	_____
碳排放	_____	零排放	_____
邮寄筒	_____	包装箱	_____
缓冲材料	_____	易碎物品	_____
环保产品	_____	环境意识	_____
道琼斯可持续发展指数	_____	联合国世界粮食计划署	_____
全球变暖	_____	人道主义援助	_____

 Our business is changing, but what hasn't changed is who we are — a trusted part of the communities we serve.

— USPS

Vocabulary

A

access /'ækses/ n. 入口，通道；v. 使用，接近，获取		U2P1
accompany /ə'kʌmpəni/ v. 伴随		U1P1
accomplish /ə'kɔmpliʃ/ vt. 完成，实现，达到目的		U6P2
accordingly /ə'kɔ:diŋli/ adv. 相应地		U4P1
accurately /'ækjuritli/ adv. 精确地		U4P1
acknowledge /ək'nɔlidʒ/ v. 承认		U4P2
acquire /ə'kwaiə/ v. 获得，得到		U6P1
acquisition /ˌækwi'ziʃən/ n. 收购		U7P1
adapt /ə'dæpt/ vt.&vi. （使）适应，（使）适合		U8P2
adhere /əd'hiə/ v. 遵循，依照		U10P1
adhesive /əd'hi:siv/ adj. 带粘性的		U2P2
n. 胶水，粘合剂		U10P1
administration /ədˌmini'streiʃən/ n. 管理，行政		U9P1
administrative /əd'ministrətiv/ adj. 行政的，管理的		U9P1
adoption /ə'dɔpʃən/ n. 采用，采纳		U5P1
advent /'ædvənt/ n. 出现，到来		U1P1
affection /ə'fekʃən/ n. 喜爱，热爱		U5P2
affordable /ə'fɔ:dəbl/ adj. 付得起的，不太昂贵的		U8P2
aggressively /ə'gresivli/ adv. 盛气凌人地		U4P2
alternative /ɔ:l'tə:nətiv/ n. 抉择，可供选择的办法		U2P2
adj. 可供替代的		U10P1
amateur /'æmətə:/ n. 业余爱好者		U5P2
ambassador /æm'bæsədə/ n. 大使		U5P1
anticipated adj. 预料的，预期的		U9P2

apparent /ə'pærənt/ adj. 明显的		U4P1
approximately /ə'prɔksimitli/ adv. 大约，几乎		U2P1
argue /'ɑ:gju:/ v. 提出理由证明，表明		U5P1
artisan /ɑ:ti'zæn/ n. 技工，工匠		U5P2
as far back as 早在……		U9P2
as opposed to (sth) 与……形成对照		U10P2
assume /ə'sju:m/ v. 呈现（某种形式）		U1P1
assuredly /ə'ʃu:ridli/ adv. 确实地，确信地		U5P1
at fault 有错误，出毛病		U4P2
authority /ə'θɔ:riti/ n. 当权者；权威		U4P2
aviation /ˌeivi'eiʃən/ n. 航空，航空制造业		U10P2
awesome /'ɔ:səm/ adj. 令人惊叹的		U8P1

B

Babylonian adj. 巴比伦的		U9P2
babysit /'beibiˌsit/ v. 照看		U3P2
back out (of) 倒出		U3P1
backup /'bækˌʌp/ n. 灾备；后援		U9P1
balance /'bæləns/ n. 结余，余额		U9P1
barcode n. 条形码		U8P2
bare /bɛə/ adj. 仅有的		U4P1
be around 出现，露面		U9P2
be aware of 意识到		U4P1
be carried away 使着迷		U5P2
be committed to 以……为己任；承诺；致力于		U8P2
be distressed about 对……感到痛苦的		U4P2
be exempt from 免于		U10P2
be good for 对……有益		U10P1
be subject to 易受……的；倾向于……的		U9P2
bilateral /bai'lætərəl/ adj. 双边的		U1P1

billboard /ˈbilˌbɔːd/ n. 广告牌 U6P2
bin /bin/ n. 箱，仓 U10P1
bio-based adj. 生物产品的 U10P1
biodegradable /ˈbaiəudiˈgreidəbl/ adj. 可以进行生物降解处理的 U10P1
bio-fuel n. 生物燃料 U10P2
biogas n. 生物气(尤指沼气) U10P2
boast /bəust/ v. 有(引以为荣的事物)，自夸 U10P2
booklet /ˈbuklit/ n. 小册子 U5P1
Braille n. 盲文字符 U9P1
brilliant /ˈbriljənt/ adj. 杰出的，非凡的 U6P1
bundle /ˈbʌndl/ n. 信把 U3P1
bundle up 捆扎，把……打包 U3P1
bureau /ˈbjuərəu/ n. 局 U1P2
buzz /bʌz/ v. (机器等)嗡嗡作响 U8P1

C

cadmium /ˈkædmiəm/ n. 〈化〉镉 U10P1
campaign /kæmˈpein/ n. 活动 U6P1
capital /ˈkæpitl/ n. 资本；优势 U5P2
capture /ˈkæptʃə/ v. 夺取，占领 U7P1
carbon /ˈkɑːbən/ n. 〈化〉碳 U10P1
cargo /ˈkɑːgəu/ n. 货物 U9P2
cartridge /ˈkɑːtridʒ/ n. 墨粉鼓 U10P1
catalogue /ˈkætəlɔːg/ n. 系列 U5P2
certified /ˈsəːtiˌfaid/ adj. 合格的 U10P1
chore /tʃɔː/ n. 家务事，杂事 U2P2
circular /ˈsəːkjulə/ n. 印制的广告，传单 U3P1
claim for 要求(赔偿) U9P2
clutch /klʌtʃ/ v. 抱住，抓住 U3P2
collective /kəˈlektiv/ adj. 集体的 U1P2
commemorative /kəˈmemərətiv/ adj. 纪念的 U1P2
community /kəˈmjuːniti/ n. 社区 U2P1
compassion /kəmˈpæʃən/ n. 同情心 U3P2
compile /kəmˈpail/ v. 收集，汇编 U9P1
complain /kəmˈplein/ v. 抱怨 U4P1
complement /ˈkɔmplimənt/ vt. 补足，补充 U8P2
complementary /ˌkɔmpliˈmentəri/ adj. 互补的，补充的 U7P2
comprehensive /ˌkɔmpriˈhensiv/ adj. 综合的，广泛的 U9P1
compressed /kəmˈprest/ adj. 压缩的 U10P1
comprise /kəmˈpraiz/ v. 包含，构成 U7P1
congestion /kənˈdʒestʃən/ n. 拥挤 U10P2
congestion charge 拥堵费 U10P2

congress /ˈkɔŋgres/ n. 代表大会 U1P2
consequence /ˈkɔnsikwəns/ n. 结果，后果 U9P2
conservation /ˌkɔnsəːˈveiʃən/ n. 保护 U10P1
conserve /kənˈsəːv/ v. 节约，节省 U7P2
consistent /kənˈsistənt/ adj. 一贯的，始终如一的 U8P2
consolidation /kənˌsɔliˈdeiʃən/ n. 整合，统一，合并 U7P1
consultative /kənˈsʌltətiv/ adj. 咨询的 U1P2
consume /kənˈsjuːm/ v. 使用，消耗 U10P1
content /kənˈtent/ adj. 心满意足的 U4P1
contingency /kənˈtindʒənsi/ n. 意外事故，偶然事件 U9P1
continuity /ˌkɔntiˈnjuːiti/ n. 连续性，连贯性 U1P2
contractor /kənˈtræktə/ n. 承包人 U3P1
convention /kənˈvenʃən/ n. 公约 U1P2
council /ˈkaunsil/ n. 理事会，委员会 U1P2
count on /kaunt/ 指望，依靠 U9P2
courier /ˈkuriə/ n. 信使，送快信的人 U1P1
courteous /ˈkəːtjəs/ adj. 有礼貌的，殷勤的 U4P2
coverage /ˈkʌvəridʒ/ n. 保险项目，覆盖范围 U9P2
covet /ˈkʌvit/ v. 垂涎，羡慕 U5P1
cradle /ˈkreidl/ n. 摇篮 U10P1
craft /krɑːft/ vt. 精巧地制作 U6P2
creation /kriˈeiʃən/ n. 创造，产生 U1P1
credit /ˈkredit/ v. 认为是……功劳，把……归于 U3P2
critical /ˈkritikəl/ adj. 紧急的，至关紧要的 U7P2
crystallize /ˈkristəlaiz/ v. 具体化，计划成型 U7P2
curbside n. 路边 U3P2
currency /ˈkəːrənsi/ n. 流通，货币 U1P1
curve /kəːv/ v. 绕弯，成曲线 U3P2
customize /ˈkʌstəmaiz/ vt. 定制，定做 U6P2

D

definitively /diˈfinitivli/ adv. 确定地，最后地 U1P1
demographic /ˌdiːməˈgræfik/ adj. 人口统计学的 U9P2
deploy /diˈplɔi/ vt. (被)采纳；(被)运用；部署 U8P2
depot /ˈdepəu/ n. 仓库，储藏所 U7P1
derive from 起源于 U5P2
destination /ˌdestiˈneiʃən/ n. 目的地 U8P1
detached /diˈtætʃt/ adj. 不偏不倚的 U4P2
devote oneself to 献身于，致力于 U5P1

devour /di'vauə/ v. 贪婪，急切地投入　　U5P2
diabetic /ˌdaiə'betik/ adj. 糖尿病患者的　　U6P1
diesel /'di:zəl/ n. 柴油　　U10P2
dimension /di'menʃən/ n. 维度，范围，规模，
　　方面　　U6P2
discard /dis'kɑ:d/ v. 丢弃　　U10P1
dispense /dis'pens/ v. 分配，派发　　U2P2
dispose /di'spəuz/ v. 处置，处理　　U10P1
diverse /dai'və:s/ adj. 多种多样的，不同的　　U9P2
document /'dɔkjumənt/ v. 用文件证明；
　　为……提供文件（或证据等）　　U9P2
domain /də'mein/ n. 领土，领地　　U1P1
domestic /də'mestik/ adj. 国内的　　U7P1
driveway /'draivwei/ n. 车道　　U3P1

E

efficient /i'fiʃənt/ adj. 有效的，效率高的　　U7P2
embark /im'bɑ:k/ v. 着手，开始从事　　U10P1
embrace /im'breis/ vt. 欣然接受　　U8P2
emerging /i'mə:dʒiŋ/ adj. 新兴的　　U7P1
emission /i'miʃən/ n. 排放物　　U10P2
emotional /i'məuʃənl/ adj. 感情的　　U4P2
engage /in'geidʒ/ vt. 吸引（注意力，兴趣）　　U6P1
engaging /in'geidʒiŋ/ adj. 有吸引力的　　U6P1
enthusiasm /in'θju:ziæzəm/ n. 热情，热心，
　　积极性　　U5P1
entrust /in'trʌst/ v. 委托（运送），托付　　U5P2
era /'iərə/ n. 时代，年代，历史时期　　U8P2
erect /i'rekt/ v. 树立，直立　　U1P2
establish /i'stæbliʃ/ v. 建立，设立　　U2P1
ethanol /'eθəˌnɔl/ n. 〈化〉乙醇　　U10P1
evolve /i'vɔlv/ vt.&vi. 演变，进化，使发展　　U8P2
execution /ˌeksi'kju:ʃən/ n. 实行，执行，
　　实施　　U6P1
expanded /iks'pændid/ adj. 扩展的　　U10P1
extend /iks'tend/ v. 延伸，扩大　　U9P1
external /eks'tə:nl/ adj. 外界的　　U10P2
extraordinary /iks'trɔ:dnri/ adj. 非常的，
　　特别的　　U1P2
extremely /iks'tri:mli/ adv. 极其地；非常地；
　　极端地　　U6P1
eye-catching adj. 引人注目的；显著的　　U6P2

F

factor in 将……纳入、列入为重要因素

（尤指作预测或计划时）　　U9P2
far more than 远不只是　　U4P1
federal /'fedərəl/ adj. 联邦的　　U1P2
fiber-optic adj. 光纤的　　U6P2
fingertip /'fiŋgətip/ n. 指尖　　U2P2
flap /flæp/ n. 门扇，封盖　　U3P1
flat-size adj. 扁平状的　　U8P2
fleet /fli:t/ n. 机群，车队　　U7P1
flip /flip/ v. 轻弹　　U8P1
formality /fɔ:'mæliti/ n. 正式手续　　U1P1
formative /'fɔ:mətiv/ adj. 形成的　　U5P1
frustrating /'frʌstreitiŋ/ adj. 令人泄气的，
　　使人沮丧的　　U4P2
fulfillment /ful'filmənt/ n. 完成，履行　　U7P2

G

gambling casino 赌场　　U9P2
gateway /'geitwei/ n. 口岸，关口　　U7P1
gear /giə/ n. （某种活动的）装备，用具　　U3P1
gender /'dʒendə/ n. 性别　　U9P2
generate /'dʒenəreit/ vt. 产生，引起　　U6P2
genuinely /'dʒenjuinli/ adv. 真正地　　U4P1
grab /græb/ v. 抓取　　U3P2
granite /'grænit/ n. 花岗岩　　U1P2
greed /gri:d/ n. 贪婪　　U3P1
grocery /'grəusəri/ n. 食品，杂货　　U2P2
guidance /'gaidəns/ n. 引导，指导　　U9P1
guilt /gilt/ n. 内疚　　U3P2
gum /gʌm/ v. 涂胶　　U5P1

H

hamper /'hæmpə/ v. 妨碍，牵制　　U1P1
hands-on adj. 动手的，实际操作的　　U10P2
harmony /'hɑ:məni/ n. 和谐　　U1P2
hassle /'hæsl/ v. 打扰，麻烦　　U4P1
head /hed/ v. 朝着……去　　U3P1
helmet /'helmit/ n. 头盔　　U3P1
high-impact adj. 重大影响的　　U8P2
historically /his'tɔrikəli/ adv. 在历史上　　U6P2
hub /hʌb/ n. 枢纽，中心　　U7P1
humanitarian /hju:ˌmæni'tɛəriən/ adj. 人道
　　主义的　　U10P2
humble /'hʌmbl/ adj. 不起眼的，粗陋的　　U5P1
hybrid /'haibrid/ n. 混合物，生成物　　U10P2
hydrogen /'haidridʒən/ n. 〈化〉氢　　U10P1

I

impact /'ɪmpækt/ n. 影响，作用	U10P1
impair /ɪm'pɛə/ v. 削弱，减少	U9P1
impetus /'ɪmpɪtəs/ n. 推动力，促进	U1P1
implement /'ɪmplɪmənt/ v. 实施；执行	U9P1
imprint /ɪm'prɪnt/ v. 把……印在……上	U5P2
in exchange for 作为……的交换	U4P1
in one's effort 在……努力下	U10P1
inaugurate /ɪn'ɔːgjʊreɪt/ v. 举行（落成）典礼	U1P2
inbound /'ɪnbaʊnd/ adj. 入境的，归航的	U7P2
incentive /ɪn'sentɪv/ n. 刺激；鼓励	U6P2
incur /ɪn'kɜː/ v. 招致	U10P2
individual /ˌɪndɪ'vɪdjʊəl/ n. 个人	U4P1
inevitably /ɪn'evɪtəblɪ/ adv. 不可避免地，必然地	U1P1
infrastructure /'ɪnfrəˌstrʌktʃə/ n. 基础设施	U7P1
initiative /ɪ'nɪʃətɪv/ n. 倡议，新方案	U10P1
inkjet n. 喷墨	U10P1
insight /'ɪnsaɪt/ n. 洞察力	U6P1
install /ɪn'stɔːl/ v. 安装，安置	U2P2
insurance /ɪn'ʃʊərəns/ n. 保险	U2P1
integral /'ɪntɪgrəl/ adj. 构成整体所必需的，不可或缺的	U10P2
integrated adj. 综合的，整合的	U7P1
interior /ɪn'tɪərɪə/ adj. 内地的，国内的	U7P1
interphone /'ɪntəˌfəʊn/ n. 内部电话，对讲机	U9P1
interruption /ˌɪntə'rʌpʃən/ n. 中断，阻碍	U9P1
intra-regional adj. 区域内的，地区内的	U7P1
inventory /'ɪnvəntrɪ/ n. 存货（清单）	U7P2
investment /ɪn'vestmənt/ n. 投资	U10P2
investor /ɪn'vestə/ n. 投资者	U10P2

K

kiosk /kɪ'ɒsk/ n. 售货亭，亭子	U2P2

L

landfill /'lændfɪl/ n. 垃圾填埋场	U10P1
landmark /'lændmɑːk/ n. 地标	U6P2
lawsuit /'lɔːsjuːt/ n. 诉讼	U9P2
lead /liːd/ n. 〈化〉铅	U10P1
leading-edge adj. （技术上）最先进的	U8P2
leak /liːk/ v. 泄漏	U10P1
legislative /'ledʒɪsleɪtɪv/ adj. 立法的	U1P2
liability /ˌlaɪə'bɪlɪtɪ/ n. 责任，义务	U9P2
liaison /lɪ'eɪzɒn/ n. 联络	U1P2
light up 照亮；使放光彩	U6P2
likelihood /'laɪklɪhʊd/ n. 可能性	U9P2
literally /'lɪtərəlɪ/ adv. 确实地，真正地	U6P2
load /ləʊd/ v. 装	U3P1
location /ləʊ'keɪʃən/ n. 地点，场所	U2P1
low blood sugar 低血糖	U3P2

M

magnify /'mægnɪfaɪ/ v. 放大，扩大	U5P2
mailshot /'meɪlʃɒt/ n. 邮寄广告	U6P1
maintain /meɪn'teɪn/ v. 保持，维持，继续	U2P2
majority /mə'dʒɒrɪtɪ/ n. 多数，大半	U2P1
manufacture /ˌmænjʊ'fæktʃə/ v. （大规模）制造，生产	U10P1
mass /mæs/ adj. 大众的；大规模的，大量的	U5P1
maximize /'mæksɪmaɪz/ vt. 最大化，增至最大限度	U6P1
maximum /'mæksɪmaɪz/ n. 最大限度，最大量	U2P2
medication /ˌmedɪ'keɪʃən/ n. 药物	U3P2
memorable /'memərəbl/ adj. 容易记忆的，值得怀念的	U6P1
mercury /'mɜːkjʊrɪ/ n. 〈化〉汞	U10P1
meticulous /mɪ'tɪkjʊləs/ adj. 极精心的，极注意细节的	U5P2
milestone /'maɪlstəʊn/ n. 里程碑；重大事件	U8P2
mist /mɪst/ n. 薄雾	U1P1
mobility /məʊ'bɪlɪtɪ/ n. 活动	U3P2
monarch /'mɒnək/ n. 君主，帝王	U1P1
monastery /'mɒnəsˌterɪ/ n. 修道院，寺院	U1P1
monopoly /mə'nɒpəlɪ/ n. 垄断，专营服务	U1P1
morality /mə'rælɪtɪ/ n. 道德；伦理	U4P1
motto /'mɒtəʊ/ n. 题词，座右铭	U1P2
multiple /'mʌltɪpl/ adj. 多样的，多个的	U9P2

N

navigation /ˌnævɪ'geɪʃən/ n. 航海，航空	U1P1
nontoxic /nɒn'tɒksɪk/ adj. 无毒的	U10P1

O

Word	Location
obsolete /'ɔbsə,li:t/ adj. 废弃的，过时的	U10P1
occasionally /ə'keiʒənəli/ adv. 偶尔	U4P2
occupation /ˌɔkju'peiʃən/ n. 职业	U9P2
on behalf of 代表	U4P2
on the eve (of) 在……前夕	U10P1
on the scene 现场	U3P2
oncoming /'ɔnˌkʌmiŋ/ adj. 迎面而来的	U3P2
operational /ˌɔpə'reiʃənəl/ adj. 可用的；操作的	U8P2
optimal /'ɔptəməl/ adj. 最佳的，最理想的	U7P2
optimisation n. (optimization) 最优化	U10P2
optimise v. 使最优化	U10P2
optimize /'ɔptimaiz/ v. 优化	U7P2
originally /ə'ridʒənəli/ adv. 原来，最初	U5P2
outgoing /'autˌgəuiŋ/ adj. 发出的，外寄的	U3P2
outlet /'autlet/ n. 营业网点	U2P1
outlying /'autˌlaiiŋ/ adj. 边远的，偏远的	U3P1
outskirts /'autˌskə:ts/ n. 郊外	U3P1
outstanding /aut'stændiŋ/ adj. 杰出的	U4P1
overdose /'əuvədəus/ v. 一次用药过量	U3P2
oversee /ˌəuvə'si:/ v. 监督，指导	U2P1

P

Word	Location
pack /pæk/ n. 包，包裹，背包	U6P1
packet /'pækit/ n. 小包	U3P1
paramedic /ˌpærə'medik/ n. 护理人员	U3P2
partner /'pa:tnə/ v. 做伙伴，同……合作	U10P1
pass on to 传递	U4P2
pass out 昏迷，昏厥	U3P2
passbook /'pa:sbuk/ n. 银行存折	U9P1
passion /'pæʃən/ n. 爱好，酷爱	U5P2
patent /'peitənt/ v. 取得……的专利权	U5P1
patron /'peitrən/ n. 顾客	U3P2
peacefully /'pi:sfuli/ adv. 平静地；和平地	U5P2
pedestrian /pi'destriən/ n. 步行者，行人	U6P2
peer /piə/ v. 仔细看，端详	U3P2
penetrate /'penitreit/ v. 渗透，穿透	U1P1
perceive /pə'si:v/ v. 感知	U4P1
perforation /ˌpə:fə'reiʃən/ n. 齿孔	U5P1
periodical /ˌpiəri'ɔdikəl/ n. 期刊	U5P2
Persia n. 波斯（西南亚国家，现在的伊朗）	U1P1
personalized adj. 个人化的；个性化的	U6P1
persuasion /pə'sweiʒən/ n. 信念，说服力，（持某一见解的）派别	U5P1
pertinent /'pə:tinənt/ adj. 恰当的；相关的	U4P2
phenomenon /fi'nɔminən/ n. 现象	U5P2
philatelic /filə'telik/ adj. 集邮的	U5P2
philatelist /fi'lætəlist/ n. 集邮家	U5P2
philately /fi'lætəli/ n. 集邮	U5P1
philosophy /fi'lɔsəfi/ n. 哲学；信条，观点	U6P1
pickup /'pikʌp/ n. 提取，揽收	U8P2
pinpoint vt. 明确指出，确定（位置或时间）；为……准确定位	U6P2
pioneer /ˌpaiə'niə/ v. 开辟，作先驱	U7P1
pledge /pledʒ/ v. 保证，发誓	U10P2
pool /pu:l/ v. 汇集，集中；共享	U9P2
pop up 突然弹出的东西，弹出式	U6P2
portable /'pɔ:təbl/ adj. 便携式的，手提的	U2P1
portfolio /pɔ:t'fəuljəu/ n. 系列产品，系列服务	U7P1
possess /pə'zes/ v. 占有，拥有	U4P1
postmark /'pəustma:k/ n. 邮戳	U8P1
precise /pri'sais/ adj. 正确的，准确的	U8P1
preconception /pri:kən'sepʃən/ n. 偏见	U6P1
pregnancy /'pregnənsi/ n. 怀孕	U9P2
premises /'premisiz/ n. 生产经营场所	U2P1
premium /'pri:miəm/ n. 保险费	U9P2
prepaid /pri:'peid/ adj.（邮资等）预先付讫的，已支付的	U5P1
prince /prins/ n. 王子	U1P1
prior /'praiə/ adj. 在前的；居先的	U9P1
privatization /ˌpraivitai'zeiʃən/ n. 私有化，民营化	U9P1
processing n. 处理	U9P1
procurement /prə'kjuəmənt/ n.（尤指为政府或机构）采购，购买	U10P2
professional /prə'feʃənəl/ adj. 专业的	U4P1
profitable /'prɔfitəbl/ adj. 有利可图的，赢利的	U6P1
prominently /'prɔminəntli/ adv. 显著地；重要地	U6P2
prompt /prɔmpt/ v. 提示；鼓励	U2P2
propose /prə'pəuz/ v. 提议，建议	U1P1
prospect /'prɔspekt/ n. 展望，愿景	U7P1
provable /'pru:vəbl/ adj. 可证明的	U9P2
punch /pʌntʃ/ v. 打孔	U5P1

purchase /'pə:tʃəs/ v. 购买   U2P2

R

ramp /ræmp/ n. 斜坡，坡道   U9P1
rather than 而不是   U4P2
reach out 伸出（手）   U3P2
reason /'ri:zn/ v. 推论；劝说   U9P2
receipt /ri'si:t/ n. 收据   U2P2
recognition /ˌrekəg'niʃən/ n. 赞誉，承认   U3P2
recruit /ri'kru:t/ v. 动员（提供帮助）   U3P2
rectify /'rektifai/ v. 纠正；改正   U4P1
redirection /'ri:di'rekʃən/ n. 改寄   U3P1
refined /ri'faind/ adj. 精炼的，精良的   U10P1
refurbishment /ri'fə:biʃmənt/ n. 翻新   U7P2
regardless of 无论；不管，不顾   U8P2
relay /ri'lei/ n. 接力，传递   U1P1
relevant /'relivənt/ adj. 相关的，切题的   U6P1
reliability /riˌlaiə'biliti/ n. 可靠性   U4P1
relief /ri'li:f/ n. 救济，救援物品   U10P2
reluctance n. 不愿意，勉强   U6P1
remittance /ri'mitəns/ n. 汇款，汇寄   U9P1
replace /ri'pleis/ v. 代替，替换   U9P2
replenishment /ri'pleniʃmənt/ n. 补充（货物）   U7P2
resilient /ri'ziliənt/ adj. 有活力的；适应力强的   U7P1
resume /ri'zju:m/ v. 重返，恢复   U3P2
retain /ri'tein/ v. 保持，保留   U6P1
retention /ri'tenʃən/ n. 保留，保持   U6P1
re-tread adj. 翻新的   U10P1
revenue /'revinju/ n. 收入，收益   U4P1
revise /ri'vaiz/ v. 修订，修正   U1P2
revolutionize /ˌrevə'lu:ʃənaiz/ vt. 使彻底变革   U8P2
roll out 推出；铺开   U8P2
rouse /rauz/ v. 唤醒   U3P2
rudimentary /ˌru:də'mentəri:/ adj. 初步的，未发展的   U1P1

S

sales pitch 兜揽生意的话，商品宣传，推销词   U6P2
scheme /ski:m/ n. 方案,设计，办法   U5P1
scissors /ski:m/ n. 剪刀   U5P1
sculptor /'skʌlptə/ n. 雕刻家   U1P2
sector /'sektə/ n. 部门   U6P1
settlement /'setlmənt/ n. 清算，结账   U9P1
shift /ʃift/ n. 变化，更替   U7P1
show off 使突出；炫耀，卖弄   U6P1
skyline /'skailain/ n. 地平线，以天空为背景映出轮廓   U6P2
slip away 溜走   U3P2
slot /'skailain/ n. 槽   U8P1
solely /'səulli/ adv. 单独地，仅仅   U9P1
sort /sɔ:t/ v. 分拣，把……分类   U3P1
source /sɔ:s/ v. 寻求（尤指供货）的来源   U7P2
species /'spi:ʃi:z/ n. 物种   U10P1
specification /ˌspesifi'keiʃən/ n. 规格，要求   U7P2
stack /stæk/ n. 堆，垛   U3P2
stakeholder /'steikˌhəuldə/ n. 利益相关者，股东   U1P2
stand out 引人注目，脱颖而出   U6P2
staple /'steipl/ n. 主题，主要内容   U3P2
station /'steiʃən/ v. 安置，驻扎   U1P1
statistical /stə'tistikəl/ adj. 统计的   U9P1
statistics /stə'tistiks/ n. 统计，统计数字   U9P2
status /'steitəs/ n. 情形，状况，状态   U8P2
steadily /'stedili/ adv. 稳定地   U1P1
stewardship /'stjuədʃip/ n. 管理工作   U10P1
sticker /'stikə/ n. 涂有粘胶的标签或纸片   U2P2
sticker /'stikə/ n. 粘贴标签   U3P1
stimulate /'stimjuleit/ v. 激发，促进   U10P2
stopover /'stɔpˌəuvə/ n. 中途停留   U7P1
strata /'streitə/ n.（pl.）阶层   U1P1
strategically /strə'ti:ʒikəli/ adv. 战略上，颇具策略地   U7P2
streamline /'stri:mlain/ v. 使……简化，使……有效率   U7P2
strive /straiv/ v. 争取，追求   U7P1
subject /'sʌbdʒikt/ adj. 易受……的；倾向于……的   U9P2
sublime /sə'blaim/ adj. 崇高的，卓越的   U1P2
submit /səb'mit/ v. 呈送，提交   U1P1
subpostmaster /səb'sidiəri/ n. 代办英国邮政业务的商店店主   U2P1
subsidiary /səb'sidiəri/ n. 子公司，分公司   U2P1
sugar-free adj. 无糖的   U6P1
summon /'sʌmən/ v. 召集   U3P2

supervise /ˈsjuːpəvaiz/ v. 监督		U1P2
supervisor /ˌsjuːpəˈvaizə/ n. 监管人		U3P2
supplement /ˈsʌplimənt/ v. 补充，增补		U9P1
supreme /səˈpriːm/ adj. 最高的		U1P2
surrender /səˈrendə/ v. 放弃，使投降		U5P1
sustainability /səˌsteinəˈbiliti/ n. 可持续性		U10P1
sympathy /ˈsimpəθi/ n. 同情		U4P1

T

take action 采取行动	U3P2
take sides 偏袒	U4P2
target /ˈtaːgit/ vt. 把……作为目标(或对象)	U6P1
telephony /tiˈlefəni/ n. 电话业务	U2P1
terabyte n. 太字节（万亿字节，缩写为TB）	U8P2
territory /ˈteritəri/ n. 领土，领域	U1P2
thereby /ˈðɛəˈbai/ adv. 因此，从而	U5P1
tire /ˈtaiə/ n. (tyre)轮胎	U10P1
toddler /ˈtɔdlə/ n. 学步的儿童	U3P2
toxic /ˈtɔksik/ adj. 有毒的	U10P1
trace /treis/ n. 踪迹，痕迹	U1P1
traffic /ˈtræfik/ n. 流量	U6P1
transaction /trænˈzækʃən/ n. 交易，业务	U2P1
transfer /trænsˈfəː/ n. 传递，转移	U10P2
treaty /ˈtriːti/ n. 条约	U1P2
trillion /ˈtriljən/ n. 万亿	U9P1
tweezers /ˈtwiːzəz/ n. 镊子	U5P2

U

unaddressed /ˌʌnəˈdrest/ adj. (信等)不写姓名地址的，无姓名地址的	U6P1
unaltered /ˈʌnˈɔːltəd/ adj. 未被改变的，不变的，照旧的	U5P1
unconscious /ʌnˈkɔnʃəs/ adj. 失去知觉的，未觉察到的	U3P2
uniform /ˈjuːnifɔːm/ adj. 一样的，相同的	U5P1
unveil /ʌnˈveil/ v. 使公之于众，公布	U10P1

V

van /væn/ n. 厢式货车	U2P1
verbally /ˈvəːbəli/ adv. 言语上；口头地	U4P2
vessel /ˈvesl/ n. 船；容器	U9P2
veteran /ˈvesl/ n. 老手，富有经验的人	U3P2
viable /ˈvaiəbl/ adj. 可行的	U5P1
victim /ˈviktim/ n. 受害人	U9P2
violence /ˈvaiələns/ n. 暴力	U3P2
visibility /ˌviziˈbiliti/ n. 能见度	U7P2
visually /ˈviʒuəli/ adv. 视觉上	U9P1
vital /ˈvaitl/ adj. 极重要的，必不可少的	U8P2

W

watch out (for) 提防，密切注意	U3P1
water-based adj. 以水为基的	U10P1
water-mark n. 水印	U5P2
whirr /hwəː/ v. 发出呼呼声	U8P1
withdraw /wiðˈdrɔː/ v. 提款	U2P2
witness /ˈwitnis/ v. 目击，见证	U3P2
wizard /ˈwizəd/ n. 奇才，精灵	U8P1

《邮政英语》教师配套资料

尊敬的老师：

您好！

为了方便您更好地使用《邮政英语》，我们特向使用该书作为教材的教师赠送配套资料。如有需要，请完整填写"教师联系表"并加盖所在单位系(院)或培训中心公章，免费向出版社索取。

北京大学出版社

教 师 联 系 表

教材名称	邮政英语		
姓名：	性别：	职务：	职称：
E-maill：	联系电话：	邮政编码：	
供职学校：		所在院系：	（章）
学校地址：			
教学科目与年级：		班级人数：	
通信地址：			

填写完毕后，请将此表邮寄给我们，我们将为您免费寄送《邮政英语》配套资料，谢谢合作！

北京市海淀区成府路205号
北京大学出版社外语编辑部　李颖
邮政编码：100871
电子邮箱：evalee1770@hotmail.com

邮 购 部 电话：010-62534449
市场营销部电话：010-62750672
外语编辑部电话：010-62767315